Mona Lisa GOD

Unravel the *Mystery* of the God of the Bible

The *Mona Lisa* GOD

Unravel the *Mystery* of the God of the Bible

Ken Tunstall, PhD

THE MONA LISA GOD
Unravel the Mystery of the God of the Bible

ISBN-10: 1-897373-61-9
ISBN-13: 978- 1-897373-61-3

Printed by Word Alive Press
131 Cordite Road, Winnipeg, MB R3W 1S1
www.wordalivepress.ca

WORD ALIVE PRESS

Acknowledgements

To Don Horban who, while he was Associate Pastor at Cedarview Community Church in Newmarket, Ontario, encouraged and supported my initial efforts to find out more about the God of the Bible.

To the experiences of life, which have taught me to have compassion for those society sees as underdogs.

To Diane Weston, who, in a discussion at a bereavement group Thanksgiving brunch, helped me better focus my target audience.

To Glenn Tunstall and Jared Westover, whose helpful feedback inspired the title of this book and identified areas needing clarification.

To Larissa Bartos at Word Alive Press, whose skilful editing gave the final manuscript a professional polish, which significantly enhanced its readability.

And finally, to the Bible, a truly inspired book, in which we're invited to reason with the God of the Bible (Isaiah 1:18) and encouraged to develop a mature faith for living (Hebrews 5:12–14).

FOREWORD

As Winston Churchill observed many years ago, "Writing a book is an adventure. To begin with it is a toy and an amusement. Then it becomes a mistress, then it becomes a master, then it becomes a tyrant. The last phase is that just as you are about to be reconciled to your servitude, you kill the monster, and fling him about to the public."[1] My wish is that the readers of this book will come to see this "monster" as was the "Beast" in "Beauty and the Beast"—not entirely without redeeming qualities.

Retired Pastor Good has noted that "Academics write books for other academics, and they write in a language and style that are almost totally inaccessible to untrained minds. Lay people, in contrast, are more apt to read Christian novels and paperback advice books on how to tap into religion's power to make one healthy, happy, and rich."[2] Suzanne Sataline of the Wall Street Journal, quoting Alan Wolfe, a professor of political science at Boston College, similarly notes that "Evangelical Protestant churches draw members by appealing to their day-to-day concerns. It's not 'hellfire and damnation' being preached, but concerns about money and social problems—a therapeutic side to faith." As well, Sataline, citing a large survey conducted by the Pew Forum on Religion and Public Life, notes that "nearly half of adults in the U.S. have switched to a faith other than the one in which they were raised or have dropped affiliation with any organized religion."[3]

This book is written by a layman for a lay audience of those who want to learn more about the being who is the God of the Bible, and His ways, in order to discover, or rediscover, a solid faith for living.

---

[1] A. Sykes and I. Sproat, *The Wit of Sir Winston* (Frewin: London, 1965), 45.
[2] J. Good, *The Dishonest Church* (Rising Star: Scott's Valley, CA, 2003), 14.
[3] Suzanne Sataline, "The Changing Faiths of America," *Market Watch*, February 25, 2008.

Preface

My interest in the Bible was catalyzed by my failures in apologetics! In social gatherings, in conversations with friends and acquaintances, and in discussions at the front door of my residence with those promoting their religious views, I was regularly frustrated by my inability to clearly articulate what I believed and craft my views into a credible and attractive position which I could soundly and comfortably maintain against the diverse propositions being put forth by others. In talking about this issue with fellow church members, including deacons and elders, I discovered that they experienced similar difficulties. Finally, I decided to do something about it.

In the spring of 1983, I expressed my frustration to Don Horban, the Associate Pastor at Cedarview Community Church in Newmarket, Ontario—the church I was then attending. My suggestion was that he should offer a course on the fundamentals of the faith to all church members. Don thought this was a worthwhile project, but instead of taking it on himself, he suggested that I do it. He said he would provide me with whatever advice I needed as well as helpful written materials. Reluctantly, but with Don's promised help, I took the project on. However, the more I delved into the subject, the more fascinated and motivated I became. I launched the twenty-week course in the fall of 1983 with good success/feedback. After several years of teaching the course, I turned it over to course alumni, Dave and Cheryl Heath.

But I was not done with the topic.

As I grew in my faith, I observed that faith in God faced negative emphases from both without and within. From without, it had become acceptable—if not fashionable—to ridicule biblically based beliefs. And from within, I observed that a pharisaical attitude was common in evangelical Christian churches and the effect of this attitude was the same as it was in Jesus' day—it kept sinners away. While I encountered many individuals whose lives exemplified salvation by grace, living a life of love, and a growing reliance on God the Holy Spirit, I did not see this as a general emphasis in the church. What I saw instead was an emphasis on good works, a rigid moral code, and a desire for human rather than divine control; in my last thirty years of church service attendance, I can recall only two pastors—Connie Gough and Mark Hazzard—who turned control over to God the Holy Spirit and abandoned their intended order of service. The result of such emphases is to drive away the very sinners the church maintains it is trying to attract.

Let me illustrate this point.

A standard evangelical maxim is "Love the sinner but hate the sin." However, what I generally observed was the elitist practice of hating both the sin and the sinner. For instance, if you are going through a divorce, if you are a homosexual, a pornographic actor, or from some other identifiable "sinful grouping" and not ready to give up that lifestyle but wanting to explore what Christianity has to offer you, most likely you will not be welcomed but rather condemned in the typical evangelical Christian church of my experience. These churches treat God's prodigals, who perhaps want to come home, like the good elder brother treated his sinful younger brother in Jesus' story of the prodigal son (see Luke 15:11–32).

However, if you are a fornicator or adulterer, it is very likely that you will be treated much better. When was the last time you heard a sermon on fornication or adultery in an evangelical Christian church? I'd opine that the reason you haven't is because fornication and adultery are all too common among evangelicals to take the political risk of preaching such a sermon. And let me make it clear that I'm *not* suggesting that sermons be preached on any specific sinful practices unless the Holy Spirit has called upon a preacher to do so. Preaching on the topic of sin in more general terms and relying on the Holy Spirit to convict people of their specific sins is, I believe, a more scriptural approach. Conviction, not condemnation, is the Christian approach to sin.

Similar views are expressed by Drew Marshall, as quoted by S. Scott: "Many look at the church and see people who seem to have it all together—and who have the same expectations of others. The broken, struggling, and unsure are tempted to steer clear. The reality is that none of us, inside or outside the church, has it all together." Scott further writes, "Marshall wants to see a heightened sense of authenticity within the church. . . . . [He says] What I've discovered is there is a massive underground church of spiritually uncoordinated and spiritually wounded people who are in the middle of deciding what to do with this Jesus they bought into so long ago. . . . . In the process of exploring these questions, Marshall has ruffled feathers . . . [but] he constantly affirms that his goal isn't to tear down. His mission is to prod the Church to think about how it can be more effective in reaching Canadians for Christ—both inside and outside of the church walls."[4]

This book is my attempt to describe the views that I see being emphasized in the Bible, hoping that the Holy Spirit can inspire their restoration. It began from a request in early 2007 by Done Karanfilis to conduct a biblically-based home study on faith.

Now let me explain the title of this book. The Mona Lisa with her famous smile is commonly seen as an enigmatic or mysterious woman. And that's how I believe most people perceive God—as an unknowable or mysterious being—the "Mona Lisa" God. But there are other analogies we can use to envision God: two that appeal to me are Winnie-the-Pooh and the Velveteen Rabbit.

Those of you who recall A. A. Milne's famous children's tales and poems about Winnie-the-Pooh may also remember that, at the end of the tale "The House at Pooh Corners," the story closes with, "But wherever they go, and whatever happens to them on the way, in that enchanted place on the top of the Forest, a little boy [Christopher Robin] and his [Pooh] Bear will always be playing."[5] But in real life, Christopher Robin would not have

[4] S. Scott, "Cutting Through the Clutter," *Decision* (Canadian edition), March 2008, 29.
[5] A. A. Milne, *The Complete Tales & Poems of Winnie-the-Pooh* (New York: Dutton Children's Books, 1992), 344.

always remained a little boy—he would have grown up and so would have discarded his beloved childhood Pooh Bear, as we all do with our favourite stuffed toys from childhood. And that's the way many of us are with God: we have a childhood faith in a "fairytale" or in a "Santa Claus" God that we discard as we mature because we've become "too grown-up" for that sort of thing.

As a young adult in university, that's what I did. I came to believe that faith in God was for the very young, the very old, and for those who really weren't too bright—and I saw myself in none of those categories. However, at the end of another wonderful children's story by Margery Williams, *The Velveteen Rabbit*,[6] that favourite stuffed Velveteen Rabbit becomes real! And 40 years into my story, God became "velveteen real" to me! So, interspersed with the story of this apparently mysterious God of the Bible is my story. My story also has a happy ending, because while I gave up on God, He never gave up on me.

If you're somewhere between a "Pooh" God and a "Velveteen" God, you're in a state that I imagine is similar to that of the trapeze artist in mid-air after she's let go of the one trapeze but before she's gotten ahold of the other. It's a scary place to be. I believe this book can help you grab onto the second God—the "real thing"—and help you remove much of the mystery surrounding your understanding of this "Mona Lisa" God.

---

[6] New York: Doubleday, 1991.

Table of Contents

1 INTRODUCTION TO THE BIBLE

Contents

Develop Perspective on the Bible

Before reading this chapter, first bring your own perspective to the topic of "The Bible" by answering the following questions.

1. What is the Bible and how did it come about?
2. What differences, if any, are there between the Protestant and Roman Catholic Bibles?
3. What does the Bible claim about itself?
4. What is the Apostles' Creed?
5. What are the most important principles for interpreting the messages of the Bible?
6. What, if any, do you see as important inconsistencies in the Bible?
7. Has anything that you've been told about the Bible in church confused you or turned you off? Explain. (e.g., arguments about the interpretation of scripture passages that end up being more confusing than helpful.)

Overview of the Chapter

- The books of both the Protestant and the Roman Catholic biblical canons are named and their origins commented upon.
- The Apostles' Creed, a capsule version of the biblical message, is presented.
- The claims for the *validity* and *consistency* of the Bible are presented. The views of ancient interpreters of the Bible on its validity and consistency are stated.

Introduction

The understanding of God provided by this book is based on the revelations about Him contained in the Bible. So let's understand something about the Bible itself before we look at what it reveals about God.

Origin and Outline of the Bible

The Bible is a collection of writings by Hebrews and early Christians about God and His ways. The 27 books of the New Testament were written in Greek by Christian apostles in the first century AD (AD is Latin for Anno Domini, "in the year of our Lord") and all 27 were first declared Christian Canon—a body of writings determined to be genuine—by Bishop Athanasius of Alexandria, Egypt, in the third century AD. The books of the Old Testament were written in Hebrew and Aramaic by inspired Hebrew prophets beginning with Moses and concluding before Christ was born as the Messiah. Roman Catholics say there are 46 canonical Old Testament Books (The Greek Septuagint Bible), based on a declaration by 70 rabbinical scholars in Alexandria, Egypt, more than 200 years BC, whereas Protestants and Jews say that there are only 39 canonical Old Testament books (The Hebrew /Aramaic Tanakh), based on a declaration by a council of Rabbis at Jamnia in Palestine, which is near Jerusalem, around 90 AD, 20 years after the destruction of the second temple in Jerusalem. I do not believe there is much theological controversy associated with the seven extra books; nevertheless, I will refer only to the Protestant Old Testament Canon. Until the 20th century, the canonical scriptures were generally accepted as true. Since then, the truth of the canonical scriptures has been frequently questioned, but different people question the veracity of different parts of the canon—there is no consensus on which scriptures are seen to be in error or not genuine. The most reasonable position is therefore the historical one: to accept all of the canonical scriptures as genuine. The canonical books of the Bible are:

NEW TESTAMENT
Matthew
Mark
Luke
John
Acts
Romans
1 Corinthians
2 Corinthians
Galatians
Ephesians
Philippians
Colossians
1 Thessalonians
2 Thessalonians
1 Timothy
2 Timothy
Titus
Philemon
Hebrews
James
1 Peter
2 Peter
1 John
2 John
3 John
Jude
Revelation

OLD TESTAMENT	
Protestant	**Roman Catholic**
Genesis	Genesis
Exodus	Exodus
Leviticus	Leviticus
Numbers	Numbers
Deuteronomy	Deuteronomy
Joshua	Josue (Joshua)
Judges	Judges
Ruth	Ruth
1 Samuel	1 Kings (1 Samuel)
2 Samuel	2 Kings (2 Samuel)
1 Kings	3 Kings (1 Kings)
2 Kings	4 Kings (2 Kings)
1 Chronicles	1 Paralipomenon (1 Chronicles)
2 Chronicles	2 Paralipomenon (2 Chronicles)
Ezra	1 Esdras (Ezra)
Nehemiah	2 Esdras (Nehemiah)
	Tobias / Tobit
	Judith
Esther	Esther (with added verses)
Job	Job
Psalms	Psalms
Proverbs	Proverbs
Ecclesiastes	Ecclesiastes
Song of Solomon	Song of Songs (Song of Solomon)
	Book of Wisdom
	Ecclesiasticus
Isaiah	Isaias (Isaiah)
Jeremiah	Jeremias (Jeremiah)
Lamentations	Lamentations
	Baruch (including Jeremiah letter)
Ezekiel	Ezechiel (Ezekiel)
Daniel	Daniel
Hosea	Osee (Hosea)
Joel	Joel
Amos	Amos
Obadiah	Abdias (Obadiah)
Jonah	Jonas (Jonah)
Micah	Micheas (Micah)
Nahum	Nahum
Habakkuk	Habacuc (Habakkuk)
Zephaniah	Sophonias (Zephaniah)
Haggai	Aggeus (Haggai)
Zechariah	Zacharias (Zechariah)
Malachi	Malachias (Malachi)
	1 Machabees
	2 Machabees

The Bible verses or scriptures that I will quote will be from the New International Version translation, unless otherwise noted. The convention that I'll follow is name of book, chapter and verses. For example, Matthew 13:1–3 refers to the book of Matthew, chapter 13, verses 1–3.

Summary of the Biblical Message

The Apostles' Creed is a statement of faith, originally written in Latin, and consistent with the Bible. This was the profession of faith that new Christian believers in the early church made before being baptized by immersion. The earliest known version dates to 215 AD in Rome, but changes were made to it over the next 700 years. These later additions are noted in **bold**. *Credo* is Latin for 'I believe [in my *heart*]'.

The Apostles' Creed

I believe in God the Father Almighty,
  Maker of heaven and earth.
And in Jesus Christ His only Son our Lord;
Who was **conceived** by the Holy Ghost, born of the
  Virgin Mary, suffered under Pontius Pilate, was
  crucified, **dead**, and buried;
He descended into hell;
The third day He rose again from the dead;
He ascended into heaven, and sitteth on the right hand
  of God the Father **Almighty**;
From thence he shall come to judge the quick [living]
  and the dead.
I believe in the Holy Ghost [Spirit];
The holy **catholic** [universal] Church;
The communion [fellowship] **of saints**;
The forgiveness of sins;
The resurrection of the body;
And the life everlasting.
AMEN.

Claims for the Bible

Here's what the Old and New Testament scripture writers claimed for the Bible.

Validity

As Jesus said, scripture cannot be broken—it is valid (John 10:35). Scripture did not come about by the prophet's own interpretation but as speaking from God when carried along by the Holy Spirit (2 Peter 1:19–21). In fact, all scripture is God-breathed or inspired by God (2 Timothy 3:16–17). Examples of God speaking to the prophets Jeremiah and John and telling them what to write—communicating scripture to them—are given in Jeremiah 36:2, "Take a scroll and write on it all the words I have spoken to you concerning Israel, Judah and all the other nations from the time I began speaking to you in the reign of Josiah till now," and Revelation 1:11, "Write on a scroll what you see and send it to the seven churches." The Old Testament is full of examples of God speaking to prophets, beginning with Moses (Exodus 24:3–4). So if God is really the source of what's written in the Bible, then what the Bible says must be valid—true and without error. This is the historical view of Bible interpreters. As Kugel states in *How to Read the Bible,* ancient interpreters of the Bible "believed that the entire Bible is essentially a divinely given text, a book in which God speaks directly or through His prophets" (15).

Consistency

The most important principle in understanding scripture is *consistency*—that the Bible does not contradict itself. If it's *true,* then of course that's what you'd expect. Again, to quote Kugel: "[Ancient] Interpreters also assumed that the Bible contained no contradictions or mistakes" (15).

So if the Bible does *appear to contradict* itself, the difficulty is in your misunderstanding and not in the biblical message itself. That being the case, do not ignore or accept the apparent inconsistency, but rather work to resolve it. The way you must resolve it is to figure out how the passages in question can all be true when they seem to say such opposite or contradictory or incompatible things. This will require you to search for, and find, the underlying consistency between the apparently contradictory passages.

Your reasoning would follow a path something like: if these passages are true and those apparently contradictory passages are also true, then what is their "lowest common denominator," the common factor that unifies them and reveals their common message? So you would begin when you encounter a passage that seems to give a different message from passages you've read elsewhere in the Bible, and then ask yourself what it would take to obtain consistency between the different passages. How might the ancient interpreters have handled these apparent differences?

The easiest way out of such a dilemma is either to state, "It's a mystery!"—an approach taken by a number of Bible interpreters over the years—or to provide an interpretation that fails to consider the meaning of a passage in the context of the rest of the Bible. However, I think the former approach is too easy a way out, and the latter is false and misleading. Accurate biblical interpretation is known as "exegesis"; literally "reading out of the text" or providing the intended meaning of the text. "Isegesis" is "reading into the text" or providing one's own personal interpretation rather than the intended meaning. The standard approach to exegesis is to consider the meaning of text in the writer's context at that time and place in history and in their particular socio-politico-cultural milieu. However, I believe biblical integrity is the most important exegetical principle. My focus has been biblical consistency in understanding the enduring truths about God, His ways, and godly living. If God is the same yesterday, today, and forever, His truths should have a similar endurance. As Isaiah 40:8b says, "[T]he word of our God stands forever."

What follows are three challenging apparent inconsistencies for interpreters.

Apparent Inconsistency #1

In Acts 4:12, Peter says, "Salvation is found in no one else, for there is no other name [than Jesus] under heaven given to men by which we must be saved." In Romans 10, Paul says, ". . . if you confess with your mouth, 'Jesus is Lord,' and believe in your heart that God raised him from the dead, you will be saved" (9) and "Everyone who calls on the name of the Lord will be saved" (13).

The typical evangelical Christian *isegetical* interpretation of these verses is that all who do not accept Jesus Christ as their personal saviour are unsaved and condemned to hell; only those who have accepted Jesus Christ as their personal saviour are saved and go to heaven. For instance, Charles Stanley, in *In Touch* magazine, states: "Only those who have received Jesus Christ as their savior will enter heaven" (36). I call this isegetical because, after you read those verses, let's say you then also read Ezekiel 18 and, when you get to verse 20, you read that only the soul that sins will die spiritually. Since you know that no one can sin before they are old enough to make a sinful choice—the age of reason—it would be isegetical to *exclude* from heaven all the *children* born before or after Christ's death and resurrection who died, or will die, before that age, even in the womb.

Using a similar line of reasoning, Acts 4:12 and Romans 10:9–13 also *exclude* from heaven all the Old Testament *heroes of the faith*; since none of these people could ever have accepted Jesus Christ as their personal saviour, *they must all be in hell*! I will speak more of this later and give an *exegetical* interpretation in chapter 4 when I discuss the process of salvation.

I believe that most, if not all, apparent inconsistencies in the Bible can be resolved by searching for, and finding, the underlying and unifying consistency.

Let me now describe two other apparent inconsistencies that I believe are the most important apparent contradictions about God in the Bible. I will show their actual consistency in the next chapter on God the Father.

Apparent Inconsistency #2

In the Old Testament, God destroys or orders the destruction of many peoples (for example Genesis 18:20–19:25 and Deuteronomy 7:16). We're also told that God is Love (1 John 4:16). *Destruction of people doesn't seem very loving*!

Apparent Inconsistency #3

We're told that God is all-knowing (Hebrews 4:13); yet God says people have freedom of choice (Deuteronomy 30:19), which seems to imply that God does *not know all* the choices that people will make, so obviously God *doesn't know everything*. Or perhaps, people don't really have freedom of choice, they only believe that they do, but God *really knows the choices* they'll make, which seems to suggest that God is *a liar*! This third dilemma apparently baffled even Albert Einstein and kept him from real faith in God.

Let's now go on to learn more about this seemingly contradictory God. But before we do, let me give one final comment about interpreting the Bible. Simply because a passage is scriptural doesn't mean it's applicable in all situations. In the fourth chapters of both Matthew (verses 1–11) and Luke (verses 1–13), Satan quoted verses from Psalm 91 to Jesus, who then rejected that scripture for His situation and instead responded with the appropriate scripture, Deuteronomy 6:16. If you use Scripture to guide your life, make sure you use biblical passages that really fit the situation!

2 GOD THE FATHER

Contents

Develop Perspective on God the Father

Before reading this chapter, first bring your *own* perspective to the topic of "God the Father" by answering the following questions.

1. Do you believe that there is a God? Why?
2. Who or what is God?
3. What do you believe about:
    a. The Trinity?
    b. God's role in creation?
    c. The possibility of God changing His mind?
4. Does God use a different approach with humankind in the Old and New Testaments? Explain.
5. What, if any, is the contradiction in the following two beliefs?
    a. God is omniscient: He knows everything
    b. People have free will
6. Is the concept of sin still relevant today? What is the difference between temptation and sin? How does temptation come about? How does sin come about?
7. Is the Devil or Satan as powerful as God? Explain why or why not.
8. Has anything that you have been told about God the Father in church confused you or turned you off? Explain. (e.g., He's inconsistent: sometimes kind and sometimes cruel; that He's male or *female*: God the Mother!)

Overview of the Chapter

There are many important topics covered in this chapter:

- It begins with a non-biblical argument for the Creator God, and then looks at ideas about gods in general in the Old Testament.
- The eight most important characteristics of God are described. Highlights of God the Father's "creator" characteristic include providing scientific evidence regarding the biblical account of creation and explaining the status of Satan, the fallen angel.
- In the section discussing the relationship of God to humankind, a resolution is proposed to the long-standing puzzle regarding God's omniscience and the free will of humankind. Arminianism and Calvinism are also assessed. In discussing sin and holiness, a number of issues are analyzed in some detail. For instance, sexual sin and divorce are examined in light of the moral primacy of love. The issues of capital punishment and abortion are discussed and the intended application period of capital punishment is defined. As well, a model is provided to explain how temptation and sin operate. Then, five causes of suffering are looked at. Death, heaven and hell, and Atheism are also discussed.
- The apparent inconsistency of God's behaviour in the Old and New Testaments is resolved.

Introduction: Evidence for God Outside the Bible

Before we look at what the Bible tells us about this apparently contradictory God, let's look at the evidence that there really is a God *apart* from what the Bible tells us.(By the way, when I use the capitalized term "God," I am referring to "God the Father," as would be commonly understood.)

Why do we even need God or a "God concept"? I struggled with this question when I was a sophomore university student taking my first philosophy course. The thing that convinced me that there must be a Creator God was something that is observable everywhere in our world—*change.* Time, the seasons, aging, human history, and the evolution of the planetary systems are all examples of change that we are aware of. All change occurs in time and therefore implies a beginning: time zero, estimated by scientists at 14 billion years ago. In terms of our physical universe, the beginning is called the "big bang" by scientists.

The obvious philosophical, but not scientific, question is What made the "big bang"? And the equally obvious answer is God, since something must have caused and created the "big bang." A well-accepted philosophical principle is that "Something [like the 'big bang'] can't come from nothing," (*ex nihilo nihil fit* in Latin). Then I might have asked, So what created God? But then I'd also have to ask, What created the Entity that created God? and What created the Entity that created the Entity that created God? and so on, ad infinitum, which becomes absurd (*reductio ad absurdum* in Latin).

So what I was forced to do was accept that there is only *one* unique Creator God who is *unchanging*—outside of time—and *different* from my world—not physical. There you go; I was stuck with God, for without God, there could be no creation.

Biblical Views on Gods in General

So what does the Bible tells us about gods in general? *All* the Old Testament peoples believed in gods—*many gods,* in fact, for they were polytheistic. For example:

- Exodus 12:12 – "the *gods* of Egypt";
- Exodus 34:11–16 – "the *gods* of the Amorites, Canaanites, Hittites, Perizzites, Hivites and Jebusites";
- Numbers 25:2–3 – Baal and other Moabite *gods*;

- Deuteronomy 7:16 – the Israelites are commanded by God to destroy the people who serve these other *gods*;
- Deuteronomy 12:2–3 – the Israelites are commanded by God to destroy the places of worship of these other *gods*;
- Joshua 24:2 – the ancestors of the Israelites worshiped other *gods*;
- Joshua 24:14–15 – the Israelites are asked to choose God over their ancestors' *gods* and the *gods* of the Amorite peoples in the Promised Land;
- Judges 2:10–19 – after the deaths of their leaders, the Israelites typically rejected the God who had led them into the Promised Land, and chose instead the *gods* of the prior inhabitants of the Promised Land;
- Judges 10:6 – some of these *gods* were Baal and the *other gods* of Aram (e.g., Rimmon), Sidon (e.g., Ashtoreth), Moab (e.g., Chemosh), Ammon (e.g., Molech) and Philistia (e.g., Dagon);
- Jeremiah 32:35 – the Israelites are rebuked by God for sacrificing—murdering—their children to appease the *god* Molech;
- Jeremiah 44:15–19 – the Israelites complain that their lives were better when they offered sacrifices to the "Queen of Heaven," who was the *goddess* Ishtar of the Babylonians.

The Old Testament peoples also believed that if you offended the *gods*, you had to appease them by atoning for your wrong-doing or offensive behaviour through making sacrifices to the *gods*—most people don't believe this sort of thing anymore. However, only the Hebrews or Jews and their ancestors believed in one unique God who *also* required atonement for sin. Let's now look at the concept of this one unique God in the Bible.

Characteristics of God

1. Unique/Trinity

- God says, "Let *us* make man in our image" (Genesis 1:26, emphasis added).
- God says to Isaiah, "Whom shall I send? And who will go for *us*?" (Isaiah 6:8, emphasis added).
- Deuteronomy 4:39, 6:4, and 32:39; 2 Kings 19:19; Isaiah 44:6, 45:5–6, 14, 21–22, and 46:9; Romans 3:30; James 2:19 and Jude 23 all tell us there is only *one* God.

So who is the "us" that God is referring to? Jesus, God the Son, sheds light on this in Matthew 28:19 when He commands His apostles to baptize people in the name of the *Father* and of the *Son* and of the *Holy Spirit*; 2 Corinthians 13:14 also refers to the members of the Trinity. When I discuss God the Son and God the Holy Spirit, I'll show that the Trinity (*Three* persons in *One* being) was also present in the Old Testament. But let me give you a "sneak preview":

1. *God the Father*: He is the omniscient and omnipotent Creator, the first among equals—*primus inter pares* (Latin)—of the Trinity.
2. *God the Son*: He is Emmanuel or "*God with us*," our Saviour/Christ/Messiah, Final Judge and High Priest, the second member of the Trinity (Micah 7:7, 18; Habakkuk 3:18; Zephaniah 3:17; John 10: 24–38; Colossians 1:19, 2:9).
3. *God the Holy Spirit*: He is our omnipresent Counsellor through His "still small voice," the third member of the Trinity (1 Thessalonians 4:8).

Since "Trinitarian" beings are not a part of our everyday experience, you may find some analogies useful in helping you imagine the Trinity. For instance, visualize the Trinity as an invisible lamp: God the Father is the invisible *energy source;* God the Holy Spirit is the *sensible manifestation* of the energy: *heat;* and God the Son is the *visible manifestation* of the energy: *light.* Or think of the Trinity as "Volume," with the members of the Trinity being *Length, Width* and *Height.* However, these are only analogies—they don't map 1:1 with the real thing.

2. Creator

Before dealing with God's role as the Creator, we need to understand the concept of truth in science and philosophy. Philosophical Science ("philosophy") is the study of all reality, and as the song says, in philosophy, pretty much "anything goes." Natural Science ("science") is the study of nature and natural phenomena—the physical universe—and in science, some things do not go. For instance, all causes in science must be physical; therefore, God cannot be a causal agent in science. When a space shuttle is launched, we'd find it strange to hear of God playing a part in helping the rocket boost the capsule into space. So it's scientific to say that the universe began with a "big bang" but it's not scientific to say that the cause of the "big bang" was God.

Parenthetically, prior to the 1920s, the dominant scientific view was the "steady state" theory, which held that the universe had always existed in, more or less, its current state. Scientists started proposing "big bang" theories in the 1920s, but it was Ralph Alpher, an American astrophysicist, who, in the late 1940s, fleshed out the "big bang" theory and is today regarded as the father of the theory. I believe it's true (philosophically) to say that God was the cause of the "big bang," but it's not science. Since people don't typically differentiate between domains of truth, the distinction is lost on them and they find it confusing that science excludes some truth.

CREATION

God created the heavens and the earth and every living thing on it (Genesis 1:1–27; Isaiah 44:18; Jeremiah 27:5, 32:17; Acts 17:24). Many scientists, including Einstein, have commented on the remarkably complex and intricate design of the universe, its unfolding, and its constituents. One small detail, as mentioned to me by Al Perttula, an engineer, is enlightening in this regard. Water increases in density until 4°C then decreases in density until 0°C—the freezing point. This means the heaviest water sinks to the bottom, permitting fish and other aquatic life to survive beneath the ice, which floats on top of the water. Philosophically, it takes more faith to believe this intricately designed universe happened by chance than by God.

EVOLUTION

An obvious question here, though, is What about evolution? Before dealing with this question, however, let's have a short refresher on evolution.

The Theory of Evolution, in which I once believed, maintains that life on earth began spontaneously in the prebiotic or primordial soup that constituted the oceans of early Planet Earth. Once formed, these early life-forms—single-cell, virus-like creatures, bacteria, etc.—evolved into more complex creatures, continuing until reaching the pinnacle of evolution: humans. This process of evolution involves the selection in nature of mutations that increase the probability of survival; the fittest survive! I'll assess separately the two key aspects of this theory: the origins of life and the evolution of species. But before I do, let me explain the reason for my prior faith in evolution.

When I was a believer in evolution, I *assumed* it was true. I thought that anyone who didn't believe in evolution was a religious simpleton stuck on the idea of God's "special creation" activity in the world and unwilling to grab onto the modern, scientific and obviously true evolutionary view that eliminated any philosophical necessity for God except at the "big bang." (And you, dear reader, may now see the writer as a religious simpleton—although perhaps an entertaining, or hopefully even a persuasive, one.)

For me, the evidence that was most persuasive in support of the theory of evolution is best captured in the saying *Ontogeny recapitulates Phylogeny.* Simply stated, it means that as the embryo develops, during its stages of development it goes through all the stages of evolution of species that lead to that particular specie in maturity. Humans, for instance, have gills in one of their earlier embryonic stages, "proving" they had fish-like evolutionary ancestors. In reality, however, ontogeny recapitulating phylogeny is a matter of faith, not fact. There is *no necessary connection* between ontogeny and phylogeny—between embryo and species development. The stages of embryo development are a matter of scientific fact and verifiable, whereas the evolution of species is a testable hypothesis but *not a matter of fact.*

Now let's assess the theory.

THE ORIGINS OF LIFE

Scientists Thaxton, Bradley and Olsen, in *The Mystery of Life's Origins*, review research, including their own, of those who have attempted to create life in conditions that simulate or enhance the conditions assumed to exist on the early Planet Earth. For scientists, their conclusions are remarkable and enlightening! They state:

> Many facts have come to light in the past three decades [1950's –1980's] of experimental inquiry into life's beginning. With each passing year the criticism has gotten stronger. The advance of science itself is what is challenging the notion that life arose on earth by spontaneous . . . chemical reactions. Over the years a slowly emerging line or boundary has appeared which shows...the limits of what can be expected from matter and energy left to themselves, and what can be accomplished only through . . . [experimenter] intervention.(185). . . . To be sure, the case for the origin of life via chemical evolution as usually presented sounds plausible, and has been accepted very widely, if not generally, by the scientific community. Furthermore, popularizations have carried the case to millions in a persuasive manner. Because of the fact that chemical evolution cannot be falsified, however, its apparent plausibility can easily

be exaggerated beyond its true status as speculation and be regarded instead as knowledge (187).

SPECIFIC EVIDENCE: CHEMICAL EVOLUTION

One of the many difficulties Thaxton, Bradley & Olsen cite for the spontaneous creation of life is the *impossibility* of excluding D- [extra, or right molecular rotation] amino acids and having only L- [aevo, or left molecular rotation] amino acids in simulations, a condition which is prerequisite for life formation in nature (52). To illustrate, naturally obtained Vitamin E is D- or *d-* or *detra*-alpha tocopherol. However, synthetic Vitamin E, produced in a lab, is DL- or *dl*-alpha tocopherol; it contains equal amounts of both the right, or natural, and left, or mirror image, molecular rotation forms because it is *impossible* to produce only the natural molecular rotation in the artificial setting of the laboratory without massive human intervention!

D. H. Kenyon, Professor of Biology at San Francisco State University, asks on page viii of the foreword to this book, "If the author's criticisms are valid . . . why have they not been recognized . . . by workers in the field? . . . Perhaps these scientists fear that acceptance of this conclusion would open the door to the possibility . . . of a supernatural origin of life."

THE EVOLUTION OF SPECIES

Johnson, in *Darwin on Trial*, highlights some of the fatal shortcomings of the theory of evolution as an explanation of the various species:

> The hypothesis . . . is that natural selection (in combination with mutation) is an innovative evolutionary process capable of producing new kinds of organs and organisms. . . . [W]hat evidence confirms that this hypothesis is true? (25) . . . None of

the "proofs" provides any persuasive reason for believing that natural selection can produce new species, new organs, or other major changes, or even minor changes that are permanent (27) . . . The prevailing assumption in evolutionary science seems to be that speculative possibilities, without experimental confirmation, are all that is really necessary (43).

SPECIFIC EVIDENCE: BIOLOGICAL EVOLUTION

Johnson, in detailing his evidence on the biological evolution of species, states:

> In a word (Darwin's word), a saltation [systematic macromutation] is equivalent to a miracle [and therefore to be avoided]. At the extreme, saltationism is . . . indistinguishable from special creation (32–33). . . . The probability of Darwinian evolution depends upon the quantity of favorable micromutations required to create complex organs and organisms, the frequency with which such favorable micromutations occur just where and when they are needed, the efficacy of natural selection in preserving the slight improvements with sufficient consistency to permit the benefits to accumulate, and the time allowed by the fossil record for all this to have happened (38). . . . [S]cience knows of no natural mechanism capable of accomplishing the enormous changes in form and function required to complete the Darwin scenario. A theory that explains only changes that have no important functional effects [normal micromutations] does nothing to solve the real mystery of evolution, which is how the marvellous molecular structures could have evolved in the first place, and how a (relatively) simple cell could change into a complex plant or animal (98–99).

For scientists like Richard Dawkins to argue that experimental confirmation of evolution is unnecessary is nonsense! Biology is not like astronomy—it is an *experimental* science.

Evolution has *never* been duplicated experimentally. The survival of intermediate species, with intermediately evolved features and organs like intermediate kidneys, livers, or limbs, is very problematic for the theory. Partially-evolved species simply won't survive—they simply aren't fit enough to survive!

> In the early nineteenth century the prevailing geological theory was the "catastrophism" advocated by the great French scientist Cuvier, the father of palaeontology. Cuvier believed that the geological record showed a pattern of catastrophic events involving mass extinctions, which were followed by periods . . . in which new forms of life appeared without any trace of evolutionary development (Johnson, 45).

The geologic/paleontological pattern is for the sudden non-transitional appearance and disappearance of species.

EVIDENCE: PALEONTOLOGICAL EVOLUTION

So what about paleontological evidence for evolution? Again, to quote Johnson:

> But what if the . . . links [necessary in the paleontological record for Darwin's theory of evolution] are missing not only from the world of the present but of the past as well? . . . What geologists . . . [have discovered] was species, and groups of species, which appeared suddenly rather than at the end of a chain of evolutionary links (46). Darwin was emphatic that the number of transitional intermediaries must have been immense (48). . . . According to Steven Stanley, the Bighorn Basin in Wyoming contains a continuous local record of fossil deposits for about five million years. . . . Because this record is so complete, palaeontologists assumed that certain populations of the basin could be linked to illustrate continuous evolution. On the contrary, . . . "the fossil record does not convincingly document a single transition from one species to the next" (51).

The obvious conclusion is that life did not, and cannot, arise spontaneously or by chance, and that species did not, and cannot, evolve into other species; on the contrary, when they appear, they are fully developed. So, how did life begin and different species come about? What about the biblically-based notions of special creation by God or intelligent design by God? These are philosophical and not scientific theories. To call "special creation" or "intelligent design" science is an oxymoron—God *cannot* be a causal factor in science.

One way to account scientifically for the known facts around the origins of life and the different species is to take a hint from the origins of the universe. The most simple and accurate scientific description is achieved by calling them the life "big bang" and the species "big bang" and, like astrophysicists, to not be concerned scientifically about what went on before the "big bang" or time zero. Interestingly, one of the most controversial topics today in astrophysics is the "anthropic principle," which "suggests that nature is the way it is simply because if it wasn't, we wouldn't be here to observe it" ("Just-Right Universe").

ADAM AND EVE

Genesis speaks of God creating a man, Adam (2:7), and a woman, Eve (2:21–22), in Eden, which was located in the Middle East, perhaps near where the Tigris and Euphrates Rivers meet in modern-day southern Iraq. Some of their sons are named but none of their daughters' names are recorded (Genesis 4:1–2, 25; 5:4, 6:2). Adam is spoken of as a literal ancestor of Jesus in Luke 3:23–38 and is described as literally the first sinner in Romans 5:12–19. But what about scientific evidence for the biblical Adam and Eve?

From the mitochondrial or non-chromosomal DNA of cells in women, which is passed down from generation to generation of women, it is known that *all women on earth are descended from a common ancestor* called *mitochondrial Eve*, based on a study published by scientists Cann, Stoneking and Wilson in 1987. The best estimate today is that she lived between 6,000 and 70,000 years ago in the area encompassing Africa, Asia Minor and the Middle East. Based on a study of the Y-chromosome of men, which is passed on from generation to generation of men, it is known that *all men on earth are descended from a common ancestor* called *Y-chromosomal Adam*, based on a study published by scientists Dorit, Akashi and Gilbert in 1995. The best estimate today is that he lived between 35,000 and 50,000 years ago in the same region as Eve. So there is genetic support for the biblical Adam and Eve in the general location and during the general timeframe suggested by the Bible, thus generally supporting where and when the Bible suggests they originated.

BIBLICAL HISTORY

Biblical accounts of events, cities, etc. are supported by archaeological findings where they exist, as noted by Govier in "Finders of the Lost Ark?" But what about support for the grand-daddy of all biblical events, the flood of Noah (Genesis 6–8)? Some of the earliest evidence for the occurrence of a massive flood came from the work of the English archaeologist Sir Charles Leonard Woolley in the 1920s while excavating near the Euphrates River. He found remnants of civilizations separated by a ten-foot thickness of clay—evidence of a massive flood. Also, geologists estimate that over seventy percent of the earth's crust is sedimentary rock—rock which has been moved by massive water movement—again giving strong evidence of a flood. There are even sedimentary rock deposits near the top of Mount Everest! The Coconino Sandstone of the Grand Canyon has been analyzed by American geologist Leonard Brand to confirm its formation by a flood. There is paleontological evidence of uprooted fossilized trees in North America and Europe, such uprootings caused by flooding. American oceanographers Cesare Emiliani and James Kennett have found evidence that there was a worldwide freshwater flood 10,000–12,000 years ago caused, they believe, by glacial melting which markedly decreased the salinity of the Gulf of Mexico, and American geologists William Ryan and Walter Pitman state that there was a catastrophic flood about 7,500 years ago around the area of the Black Sea caused by melting glaciers, with the Mediterranean flooding into the Black

Sea. Again, the biblical account of world-wide flooding is supported by scientific evidence!

The Angels

The angels are spirit creatures—beings created by God— who are mentioned many times in the Bible (for instance, at the birth of Jesus in Luke 1:26–38, 2:8–15). The Devil (also referred to as Satan or Lucifer) is also an angel who, along with the other angels who became evil, was kicked out of heaven and into hell (Luke 10:18, Matthew 25:41, Revelation 12:7–9). Satan's origins and fall are described in Isaiah 14:12–15 and Ezekiel 28:12–15. His power limitations are best described in Job 1:6–2:10. God and Satan are *not* equals, with God being the god of Good, and Satan the god of Evil. Satan is a creature, not a god, who can do no evil unless *permitted by God*, and Satan is unable to accomplish his evil purposes through people unless people *give in to his tempting*. Satan tempted Jesus (Luke 4:1–13, Hebrews 4:15), Judas (John 13:21–30, Matthew 27:1–5), and Peter (Luke 22:31–34, 54–62). Wonderfully, God promises that He will not allow us to be tempted beyond what we are able to handle, and when we are tempted, He will always provide a way out (1 Corinthians 10:13). If you ever feel you *are* being tempted beyond what you're able to handle, just call out to God for help and you'll get it! I'll say more about understanding temptation and sin in the next section: The Relationship of God to Humankind.

3. Spirit

God is Spirit (Genesis 1:1–2, John 4:24, 2 Corinthians 3:17).

4. All-Knowing/Omniscient

God knew my life path before I was born (Psalm 139:16); His understanding is unlimited (Psalm 147:5); only God the Father knows the time of the end of the world (Matthew 24:36); and nothing is hidden from God (Hebrews 4:13).

5. Always Everywhere/Omnipresent

God sees us everywhere (Psalm 139:7–12, Proverbs 15:3) and God is always everywhere (Jeremiah 23:23–24).

6. All-Powerful/Omnipotent

He is the Almighty God—in Hebrew, *El-Shaddai* (Genesis 17:1, Exodus 6:3).

7. Constant/Unchanging

God is eternal (Genesis 21:33—in Hebrew, *El Olam*) and everlasting (Psalm 90:2). God does not change (Psalm 102:27, Malachi 3:6). Jesus Christ—God—is the same yesterday, today, and forever (Hebrews 13:8).

Regarding Jesus, how can He be the *same* yesterday, today, and forever when Luke 2:52 says that He "*grew* in wisdom and stature, and in favor with God and men" (emphasis added)? From a consistency viewpoint, the simplest interpretation of these two passages is that Jesus the *man* had increased access to His *godly* wisdom as He grew physically. God the Son *did not learn* as He grew; rather, Jesus the man *tapped increasingly into His godhood* as He grew.

God's name is "I AM" (Exodus 3:14), a name that Jesus claimed for Himself (John 8:58). It is not "I WAS" or "I WILL BE," but "I AM." God is in the eternal present. For God, *all of eternity is now*! That's why God is unchanging—the same yesterday, today, and forever—because He is eternally immanent, or always now. In other words, God does not have to remember or ponder or think about or learn things because He knows it *all in the eternal present*!

The analogy which has helped me gain a more intuitive understanding of God's "eternal immanence" uses the concepts of "space" and "time." Let me restrict "space" initially to Planet Earth; now let's bring "time" in. When it's noon GMT, it's 8 a.m. in New York, 7 a.m. in Chicago, 6 a.m. in Calgary, 5 a.m. in Los Angeles, 4 p.m. in Moscow, 8 p.m. in Singapore, 9 p.m. in Tokyo, and midnight in New Zealand—but as far as Planet Earth is concerned, it's all the same time. If I could see the planet from a space capsule, I would see it all at the same time. In other words, *all* of earth space is captured by the moment in time in which I view it.

Now let's push the analogy up one level. Instead of imagining "space," imagine "space-time" and then add to it the "spiritual" dimension. Just as all of earth can be seen at a moment in time from a space capsule, God the Father can see *all* of space-time—the Universe since the "big bang"—in His spiritual "always now"! God the Father began space-time at the "big bang," God the Son paid a 30-year redemptive visit to space-time over 2000 years ago, and God the Holy Spirit has always been available for counsel in space-time since people arrived, but the Trinity has always been eternally immanent in the realm of the spirit. Tolle, in *The Power of Now*, describes a number of approaches to being fully present that can enable us humans to gain some small insight into the immanence of God.

To try and understand "being eternally present" in human terms means that, *before time began*, God knew *all* that would ever happen throughout *all* of time. For God to not know it all, as in to have to learn or to actually be surprised by something, means that God would change. But if God changes, God is *not* unchanging—the same yesterday, today and forever. This would mean that God had a beginning, that God is really a *creation,* that another being created God. But God *is* unchanging! So God *always* knew the following *possibilities*: that Satan and other angels would sin, that Adam and Eve would sin, that the world at the time of Noah would be exceedingly wicked, and that all people would eventually sin. That's why we needed a Saviour! God the Father, God the Son and God the Holy Spirit *all existed before time began*! God the Son being born in human form as Jesus over 2,000 years ago to be our Emmanuel or "God with us" was always part of God's plan, since God knew the possibility that we'd all eventually sin. (Chapter 4 also explains that Jesus' birth was *not* the beginning of God the Son here on earth.)

WHAT IS GOD LIKE?

People like to humanize God just like they do their pet animals. When you look at paintings supposedly depicting God the Father, God is always portrayed as an old man. But God is neither man nor woman and has neither penis nor vagina, though Jesus called Him "Father" and one of His names, *El-Shaddai* (Genesis 17:1, Exodus 6:3), literally means "the god with breasts" in Hebrew. To try and get your human mind around a Being who always was, is, and always will be, and who knew all the possibilities of history from the beginning to the end from before time began—with *no* mistakes—is incomprehensible to our human minds! God is truly unique in His awesomeness!

ANTHROPOMORPHISM

"Anthropomorphism" is the practice of "humanizing" or attributing human qualities to things that are not human. We commonly do this with pets, which are considered, for instance, to be "members of our family." However, whether we make them members of our family or not, pets are *not* human. Similarly with God, we want to give Him human qualities, but God is *not a human being* (Deuteronomy 4:15–18).

My favourite human quality attributed to God is that He is said to be "slow to anger and abounding in love" (Nehemiah 9:17; Psalm 103:8, 145:8; Joel 2:13; Jonah 4: 2). The human quality attributed to God that I like the least is when His anger is said to "burn" against people (Exodus 4:14; Numbers 11:10, 12:9, 22:22, 25:3, 32:10; Deuteronomy 31:16-18; Joshua 7:1; Judges 2:12-14, 20, 3:8, 10:7; 2 Samuel 6:7, 24:1 and many other places in the Old Testament). The only place where God's anger is mentioned in the New Testament is in Mark 3:5, where Jesus the man looked at the religious Jews in anger. He was deeply distressed at their stubborn hearts as they judged the healing of the man with a shrivelled hand as work, rather than as doing good, on the Sabbath.

When people experience emotion, it changes them. If we're angry, fearful or sad, we're different—changed—from when we're calm and at peace or in some other emotional state. That being said, let's now consider the Old Testament passages that speak of "God's anger" in the context of God "*never changing*." From a consistency perspective, we can humanize God and allow that He changes, or we can affirm His always being the same and accept that the scripture writers also *anthropomorphized* God. Personally, I prefer to believe that God never changes. As Numbers 13:19 states, "God is not a man."

On a related subject, we can see that God had empathy with the Old Testament conceptions of the physical world. For instance, in Job 38 God mentions: "laying the Earth's foundation" (4-6), "the storehouses of snow and hail" (22), and rain from the "water jars of heaven" (37). God's purpose in inspiring the Bible was to communicate about Himself and His ways to people. If it takes anthropomorphic or empathic metaphor to achieve that end, so be it! God's "anthropomorphized anger" communicates that certain behaviours lead to hell and away from heaven and, for us humans, that is of eternal critical importance.

MY GOD

People also like to "own" God. They speak of "my" God or "our" God, but God belongs to no one. Before there was a Muslim, Christian, Hebrew/Jew or any human being, there was God! It is presumptuous at best, and arrogant at worst, to claim ownership or exclusive relationship to God. God is the loving Father of all humankind, *bar none* (see Jeremiah 32:27)!

8. Holy and Loving

God says that He is holy (Leviticus 11:44–45, 19:2). Holy means both "whole or complete" and "spiritually or morally perfect: free from evil or sin." God speaks of His love for Israel in Jeremiah 31:3 and Hosea 3:1; Jesus tells us about God's love for all of humankind in John 3:16; and finally, the Apostle John tells us that God is Love in 1 John 4:16.

Relationship of God to Humankind

The major logical conundrum of the Christian faith revolves around the issue of people's *free will* (you can make choices that are *not* predetermined) and God's *omniscience* (He knows *all*). Eldredge states the common Christian view in *Wild at Heart*: "Trying to reconcile God's sovereignty [omniscience and omnipotence] and man's free will has stumped the church for ages" (32). The two most widely accepted Protestant Christian views of our relationship to God are Calvinism and Arminianism; both are commented on in Olsen's referenced article.

Arminianism

The Arminianist position is that people choose God; by a free act of will, people choose the way of sin or the way of holiness. The five key points of this *Free Will* doctrine are as follows:

1. *The Free Will of People*: People can either accept or reject the call of God; our choice of God's way precedes salvation.
2. *God's Grace can be Resisted*: Those called by God can resist; God's grace can be resisted by people's free will.
3. *The Conditional Election of the Called*: Election is conditional upon people's free choice; God does not play favourites.
4. *The Universal Redemption of the Elect*: All of humankind can be saved; only those who choose God's way are actually saved.
5. *The Falling from Grace of the Saints*: The saved can fall from grace; salvation can be lost through unrepented sin.

As you can see, free will is *key* in Arminianism, but God's omniscience seems compromised since it seems He may not know who will and who won't be saved.

Calvinism

The Calvinist view is that God predestines, or designates, the people who will lead a righteous life and be saved. The five key points of this doctrine of *Predestination* are as follows:

1. *The Total Depravity of People*: People are too inherently corrupt to choose righteousness; God gives people the faith to believe in Him.
2. *The Irresistible Grace of God*: Those called by God cannot resist; God's grace is invincible.
3. *The Unconditional Election of the Called*: The called have no special merit; they are God's arbitrary choice.
4. *The Particular Redemption of the Elect*: The people *not* called by God cannot be saved; only the elect are redeemed.
5. *The Perseverance of the Saints*: Redemption is eternal; salvation cannot be lost.

As we can see, free will plays *no* role in Calvinism; God's omniscience and omnipotence are key.

Since Calvinism is so different from Arminianism, I'll examine three of its foundational passages, found in Romans 8, 9, and 11, from both a consistency and a direct interpretation viewpoint.

Romans 8:29–30

"For those God foreknew [would be saved as opposed to *those He foreknew would not be saved*] he also predestined to be conformed to the likeness of his Son. . . . And those he predestined, he also called; those he called, he also justified; those he justified, he also glorified." In John 3:16, Jesus states "For God so loved the world [*everyone*] that he gave his one and only son, that *whoever* believes in him shall not perish but have eternal life" (emphasis added). Let me again twice quote Paul, first from Romans 11:32, "For God has bound *all* men [people] over to disobedience so that he [God] *may have mercy on them all*" (emphasis added), and secondly from 1 Timothy 2:3, "This is good, and pleases God our Savior, who wants *all men* [*people*] to be saved [emphasis added]." Also, Peter writes in 2 Peter 3:9b, "He is patient with you, not wanting anyone to perish, but *everyone* to come to repentance" (i.e., be saved; emphasis added).

Clearly, from the perspective of consistency, *salvation is open to all.* It is particularly fitting that Paul, after having written Romans 8:29–30, states that God wants *all people* to receive God's mercy and be saved (also see Revelation 22:17).

Romans 9:14–24

Calvinists will argue that these verses show that the saved are God's *arbitrary* choice, but this is an *incorrect* interpretation of these verses. Rather, they show that God does not have to *account* to anyone for those who are saved or unsaved—which is obvious, because He is God! And "not having to account" doesn't mean that God is *inconsistent* or *arbitrary*, it simply means that *He does not have to justify Himself*! We see this clearly in the case of Job 38–41, where God does not *explain* to Job His "unfairness" toward him but merely reminds him that He is God. However, this "unfairness" does not imply that God has removed either His love or His salvation—His favour—from Job, as chapter 42 shows us. Jeremiah 18:5–10 wonderfully clarifies the way of God described in Romans 9:14–24.

> Then the word of the Lord came to me: "O house of Israel, can I not do with you as this potter does [shaping the clay as it seems best to him]?" declares the Lord. "Like clay in the hand of the potter, so are you in my hand, O house of Israel. If at any time I announce that a nation or kingdom is to be uprooted, torn down and destroyed, and if that nation I warned repents of its evil, then I will relent and not inflict on it the disaster I had planned. And if at another time I announce that a nation or kingdom is to be built up and planted, and it does evil in my

> sight and does not obey me, then I will reconsider the good I had intended to do for it."

These verses show us that God is *not* arbitrary, but:

1. *consistent*—the same yesterday, today and forever,
2. wants *none* to perish, and
3. shows *everyone* His way, which involves repentance and leads to salvation.

Given these truths about God and His ways, to imply that the saved are God's *arbitrary* choice is to *negate* the *consistency* of the truths that God has given to tell us the way we can take in order to be saved, never mind His exhortations to us to choose that way. It is nonsense to negate these truths! Rather than leaving us in the hands of a *consistent* Loving God, it appears that the Calvinists wish to saddle us with a *capricious* and mysterious "Mona Lisa" God!

Romans 11:29

"For God's gifts and his call are irrevocable." Calvinists interpret this to mean that God cannot "re-call" or take back His call and that people cannot resist His call. However, they are wrong on both counts. For instance, God called Saul to be the first king of Israel, but later withdrew the honour and instead called David to be king (1 Samuel 10:1–16:14). Also, the passage does not even imply that people cannot resist God's call. It does not say that our response to God's call is irrevocable, it simply says that God's call to us is irrevocable—that He will forever want each person on the face of this earth to seek His salvation, as Romans 11:32 cited above implies.

Commentary

If you are a Calvinist, you're a firm believer in God's omniscience. Well, if that's the case, do you imagine that the Holy God of Love would deliberately create people destined for hell? Do you imagine that He only loves those He created to be saved and then created people He did not love who are destined to be unsaved, or, even worse, that He created people that He did love whom He destined for hell? If that's the case, that leaves a pretty big gap in God's love and holiness.

Some have tried to argue that in foreknowing those who will or won't be saved, God's behaviour is analogous to that of a cosmic weather forecaster, as in "foreknowing" meaning He only *forecasts* those who will and won't be saved. But God is not only the cosmic meteorologist, He's also the cosmic weather-*maker*. To believe that God made people whom He predestined for hell is to make God out to be a cruel monster who outdoes Satan with respect to evil, which is nonsense! So, the only reasonable interpretation of Romans 8:29–30, 9:14–24, and 11:29 is that God not only foreknows the life path of *all* of humankind, but that He has also allows in his plans for humankind that *all* may choose the path of repentance and be saved. And, as noted above, this interpretation is consistent with Jeremiah 18:5–10, John 3:16, Romans 11:32, 1 Timothy 2:3, and 2 Peter 3:9. Interestingly, the historic Roman Catholic position is more similar to Arminianism than to Calvinism.

Conclusion

Calvinism and Arminianism are so diametrically opposite positions that they obviously cannot both be true. In the context of Romans 8:29–30, 9:14–24, 11:29, and Ephesians 1:1–14, the Calvinist position has obvious merit. However, in the context of the entire biblical message, it is an *isegetical* position. Calvinism is massively *inconsistent* with the overall message of scripture. And the Calvinism–Arminianism debate is not some mere academic or intellectual exercise: people's immortal souls are put at stake here! If, as I've shown, the Calvinist position is false—untrue—a lie, we know that its ultimate source is Satan, the Father of Lies!

Dilemma

To return again to the Omniscience-Free Will dilemma, it seems we can preserve God's omniscience but give up people's free will, or else we can preserve our freedom of choice but admit that God doesn't know everything. God, as we saw earlier, is the loving Creator of everything that exists, and He is omnipresent (is everywhere all at once), omnipotent (all-powerful), and omniscient (all-knowing). The Bible also tells us that people are free to choose to do either good or evil; in fact, in Deuteronomy 30:11–20 and in many other places in the Bible, God exhorts people to choose good—and *life* everlasting—over evil and *spiritual death* in eternity. It would be a monstrous deception if God asked people to choose eternal life but made them unable to do so.

So people are free to choose to do either good or evil. The conundrum is as follows: if God knows all, then He knows what choices people will make, so people are not *really* free, only *apparently* so (i.e., even though we don't usually *feel* compelled in the choices we make, God does *know* what those choices will be). Alternatively, if God doesn't know the choices we'll make, then He doesn't know all. A dilemma! So what's the answer? The answer depends on our conception of God's knowledge. This is an application of the *consistency principle* discussed in chapter 1.

God's Knowledge: The Train Track Analogy

If God knows all the choices we'll make, then our moral life is like a train running along the tracks with the switches, or theoretical choice points, already set to the God-ordained path. Whatever it might *feel* like, our choices are apparent, not real. Just as you can know where a train will end up just by knowing where the tracks go and how the switches are set, so God knows where we're going and where we'll end up because He created us and set us in motion on the track of our pre-ordained life with all the switches, or choices, preset.

If this view is correct, then people are *not* free to choose, and so, we are *not really free*. In effect, this view says God created us as robots, which is very counterintuitive to us humans and, it seems to me, very disrespectful of God's creation of humankind. But God says we *are* free to choose, so there must be *another way of looking at free will.*

The "train track" logic, then, is this:

a. God says people have free will/can choose,

b. but God knows all the choices people will make;

c. therefore, God is a *liar.*

God's Knowledge: The Decision Tree Analogy

A decision tree is a path with many choice points along it, the different choice points themselves leading to different paths and additional choice points. If our lives are like decision trees, this implies that God knows all the choices we *might* make or have available to us, but not the moral choices we will *actually* make. Hence, the choices we make along our decision tree life path are *solely ours.*

Doesn't this imply that God is not all-knowing? No, because God knows *all our possible* choices, and so, is *never surprised* by our *actual* choices! As you can imagine, the knowledge required of a "decision-tree" God is infinitely greater than that required of a "train track" God. This is in the spirit of what is known today as "Open Theism."

So what we must do is accept a different paradigm for "God knows everything." "Everything" means "all the possibilities"—all the possible choices that people *might* make—and not "all the actualities"—all the actual choices that people *will* make. These actual choices are unknowable because we have free will. A God of "possibilities" requires much greater knowledge than a God of "actualities"!

CHOICES ALLOWED BY GOD (DECISION TREE)

Let me cite some biblical examples that illustrate people making divinely-allowed choices with respect to their life decision trees.

1. The Sun

Joshua got God to stop the sun at mid-day for one full day (Joshua 10:12–14). But an omniscient God would have already known of the possibility that Joshua would make such a request, and so allowed for that possibility.

Hezekiah, through Isaiah's prayerful intervention, got God to send the sun backwards ten steps (2 Kings 20:8–11, Isaiah 38:7–8). In His omniscience, God would have already known that possibility.

Obviously, in both these instances, one alternative choice for which God would have allowed was for the sun to continue on its normal course. I have read that these biblically recorded incidents account for a historical anomaly in the sun's path across the sky.

2. Life Extension

God had a certain life-plan in mind for Hezekiah—his life was to end because of illness—but He let Hezekiah make the choice to extend his life. God gave an additional 15 years of life in answer to Hezekiah's prayer, to the detriment of the kingdom of Judah (2 Kings 20:1–18). Clearly, in addition to his death, God would have had allowed for the possibility of Hezekiah's life-extension choice in the decision tree for his life (Isaiah 38:1–6).

3. Punishment for Israel's Sinfulness

God twice relented from punishing the nation of Israel in response to the prayer of Amos (Amos 7:1–6). In these two incidents, God again does not change His mind but instead permits Amos to make a choice for Israel of which He was well aware. God had already allowed for this alternative to punishment through the intervention of Amos in the destiny of the Nation of Israel.

> Proverbs 16:9 states: "In his heart a man plans his course, but the Lord determines his steps." I interpret this to mean that the various "steps" in our lives—the choices available to us—are established by God, but the "course" we take—our *actual* choices—are determined by *our* decisions. Similarly, Jeremiah 6:16 states: "This is what the Lord says: 'Stand at the crossroads and look; ... ask where the good way is [what decision tree branch to take], and walk in it, and you will find rest for your souls.'"

The "decision tree" logic, then, is this:

a. God says people have free will/can choose

b. and God knows all the possible choices *available* to us but not the *actual* choices we will make, so our actual choices can *never surprise* God;

c. therefore, God has told us the truth.

So we can see that God *is* all-knowing and people *are* free moral agents.

Sin and Holiness

What are some of the holy or sinful choices that people can make? Holy choices are those God wants you to make and sinful choices are those that God would rather you *not* make; holy choices involve obedience to God and sinful choices involve disobedience to God; holy choices are what's *best* or most loving for yourself and others and sinful choices are what's *bad* or unloving for yourself and others. But God is not some celestial killjoy. He made us, knowing what would work best for us; we are the people of His design.

By that standard, you'd think that God would have been most pleased with the Pharisees. In Philippians 3:5–6 Paul the apostle describes his life as Saul the Pharisee prior to his conversion: "[C]ircumcised on the eighth day, of the people of Israel, of the tribe of Benjamin, a Hebrew of Hebrews; in regard to the law, a Pharisee; as for zeal, persecuting the [Christian] church; as for legalistic righteousness, faultless." After gaining a relationship with Christ, he described himself as "not having a righteousness of my own that comes from the law [obeying the 613 commandments contained in the first five books of the Old Testament], but that which is through faith in Christ—the righteousness that comes from God and is by faith" (Philippians 3:9).

Moreover, it's not just Paul who rejected legalistic righteousness, Jesus did too. In fact, Jesus reserved His harshest criticisms for the legalistically righteous rather than the self-confessed sinners. He calls the Pharisees hypocrites, sons of hell, blind guides, blind fools, blind men, snakes, and a brood of vipers (Matthew 23:13–36). He tells them, "[O]n the outside you appear to people as righteous but on the inside you are full of hypocrisy and wickedness" (28) and "You give a tenth [tithe] of your spices—mint, dill and cumin. But you have neglected the more important matters of the law—justice, mercy and faithfulness. You should have practiced the latter, without neglecting the former" (23). So, while supporting commandments on tithing,[7] Jesus emphasized that other things, such as justice, mercy, and faithfulness, were more important. Before we try to understand how people working so hard at being righteous could screw it up so badly (fully explained in the introduction to chapter 5), let's try to better understand some of the 613 commandments.

The 613 Commandments of God

Rabbis have determined that God gave Moses 613 commandments to show the Hebrews how to live righteously. All 613 are contained in the Torah or Pentateuch: Genesis, Exodus, Leviticus, Numbers, and Deuteronomy. The ten best known commandments are in Exodus 20:3–17 and Deuteronomy 5:5–21:

1. Have no gods before God—He is to be your only god;
2. Make no idols for worship;
3. Do not use any of God's names as a profanity;
4. Make the Sabbath a holy day of rest;

[7] Tithing refers to giving ten percent of one's income or produce to God's work.

5. Honour your parents;
6. Do not murder or intentionally kill another person;
7. Do not commit adultery—only married people are to have sex and only with their spouse;
8. Do not steal;
9. Do not give false testimony or lie under oath; and
10. Do not covet or envy anything that others have.

Sex

There are commandments against other sexual sins besides the seventh, adultery, including: incest, or sex with relatives (Leviticus 18:6-18); sex with women during their menstrual period (Leviticus 18:19); sodomy, or male anal sex (Leviticus 18:22); bestiality, or sex with animals (Leviticus 18:23); and fornication, or unmarried sex (Numbers 25:1–8). Female homosexual sex is not a specifically named sin in the Old Testament but is alluded to as a sinful practice in the New Testament in Romans 1:26. Any abuse of children, sexual or otherwise, is condemned by Jesus in the strongest terms in all three synoptic gospels (Matthew 18:5–6, Mark 9:42, Luke 17:1–2).

Parenthetically, I would note that to *be* a homosexual is *not* a sin; the named sin is male homosexual sex. Today, the most popular belief about homosexuality is that it is an inherited tendency. Up until 1973, the American Psychiatric Association classified homosexuality as mental illness, with the typical aetiology in males involving a weak or absent father and a domineering or abusive mother. If you are a homosexual, wondering if your sexuality is genetic or developmental, and would like to resolve the issue for yourself, I'd recommend finding a non-homophobic heterosexual counsellor who is willing to help you explore and work through the issue. See also Appendix 1: Homosexuals.

By the way, I'd note that, according to the Bible, it's not only homosexual sex that's sinful; all heterosexual sex is *also* sinful, save that between husband and wife outside of her menstrual period. So why does God make such a big deal about sex? I believe that it's because sex has such a powerful impact on us. Genesis 2:24 speaks of a very intimate, or "one flesh," relationship between a man and a woman. But sex doesn't only constitute an intimate relationship, it's also a very pleasurable act, so it's easy to get caught up in the pleasure and forget about the intimacy. But sex *is* an intimate relationship. I believe we mess ourselves up both emotionally and spiritually by focussing only on the pleasurable aspects.

There's an analogy one can make between sex and eating. Just as sex has both intimacy and pleasure associated with it, so eating has both nutrition and taste—oral and olfactory pleasure—associated with it. In the past, unhealthy food was stale or mouldy and looked unappealing or had an unpleasant taste or odour. Today, however, since people have learned to make non-nutritious food tasty using salt, fat, spices, and sugar, we have an obesity epidemic. So, just as we need nutrition linked with taste for healthy eating, we need intimacy coupled with pleasure to maintain the fully human quality of the sexual act between a man and a woman.

Dube cites Holt-Lunstad, who finds the health benefits of marriage only accrue in relationships having "a greater level of ... intimacy." Years ago, I learned of a Colorado judge who found that juvenile delinquency also increased in the absence of parental "loving intimacy"—children feel insecure in a home where the parents don't love each other. I also learned about a process of relationship development from an audiotape presentation by Terry Gorski, a recovery counsellor. This process helps in the maintenance of that intimacy focus. The five recommended steps of relationship development, which are based on my interpretation and enhancement of Gorski's process, are:

1. Awareness – You become aware of, and are attracted to, another person.
2. Activity – You begin the relationship by doing things together in order to become better acquainted with the

other person. This helps you to more fully understand and appreciate them. But, at least initially, the activity may be more important than the person (e.g., if the other person doesn't want to see the movie that interests you, you may ask someone else to go with you).

3. Friendship – This is now a person you like and whose company you enjoy. You *want* to spend time with *this* person! So, for instance, if this person doesn't want to see the movie that interests you, you look for something else that the two of you can do together.

4. Intimacy – You share intimate, personal details with this person whom you have come to trust and love. This may include fears, hurts, hopes and dreams, disappointments, life goals, etc. If you have sex at this stage it is still a sin, but at least you're having sex with a friend who you love and not just some "hottie."

5. Commitment – You wish to make a life-long commitment with your intimate friend. In other words, you decide to marry.

Stanley and Iris is a Hollywood movie that illustrates this five step process. The movie beautifully depicts the evolution of the relationship between the "Stanley" character, played by Robert DeNiro, and the "Iris" character, portrayed by Jane Fonda, from awareness through to commitment.

Incidentally, I would also note that masturbation is not sin unless done with lust for another person. Onanism has been used to classify masturbation as sin but this is bogus. Onan's sin was his unwillingness to have children with his dead brother Er's wife Tamar, who he obligatorily married after his brother Er's death. Their children would have been considered as belonging to Er, so to avoid that possibility, Onan withdrew his penis during intercourse with Tamar and ejaculated outside of her (Genesis 38:1–10, cf. Deuteronomy 25:5–6).

Jesus linked lust with commandment #7, adultery (Matthew 5:27–28), and anger with #6, murder (Matthew 5:21–22). He was more concerned with the *intent* of the law and the character traits underlying it than the *letter* of the law.

Key

In fact, Jesus consolidated all 613 commandments into two:

1. "Love the Lord with all your heart and with all your soul and with all your mind. This is the first and greatest commandment" (Matthew 22:37–38, taken from Deuteronomy 6:5).
2. "And the second is like it: 'Love your neighbor as [you already love] yourself.' All the Law and the Prophets hang on these two commandments" (Matthew 22:39–40, taken from Leviticus 19:18).

Clearly, to do what's loving for yourself and others is to do what's best for yourself and others.[8] God doesn't want to rob you of joy; He wants to see you take the joyful path in life. If you love yourself, you won't sin against yourself, and if you love others, you'll do the same for them and, for instance, obey those of the ten commandments that apply to others: #6 murder, #7 adultery, #8 theft, #9 lying about others, and #10 coveting what belongs to others (Romans 13:8–10). And to ignore your neighbour—those others you meet whom you could reasonably be expected to help or do good for—can cause God to reject you, as the passage on the sheep and the goats explains (Matthew 25:31–46).[9]

Divorce

So what about *divorce*? How do the two love commandments apply here? In Malachi 2:16 God says He hates divorce, and Jesus said divorce was wrong except on the grounds of adultery (Matthew 5:31–32). In 1 Corinthians 7:15 Paul added the grounds

[8] The role of love is fully examined in chapter 5.
[9] The "sheep and goats" passage is fully explained in chapter 4 under "The Process of Salvation."

of an unbeliever who deserts their spouse. Mart De Haan, in his referenced work, quotes the advice given to a woman about divorce in a marital situation where she sees herself as being abused: ". . . without evidence of an affair or the abandonment by an unbelieving spouse, [a wife] doesn't have biblical grounds to leave her husband. The same church leaders have told her that separation is not an option because it is often the first step to a divorce." However, divorce, like any other sin, is subsumed under Christ's two commandments of love (Matthew 22:37–39). If you allow yourself to be abused in a marriage, you are not loving yourself, and that is the greater sin! A note of caution, however. Even if the choice to divorce is the loving one for the person making the choice, its effect on that person and their spouse is likely to be very painful, and the effect of divorce on the children of divorce will most probably be devastating!

HOW I WAS AFFECTED BY TWO DIVORCES

I did not have a personal relationship with God in my first marriage. During the final years of the marriage, I was severely depressed: I only looked forward to work on weekdays, weekends with my two children, and the escape that sleep brought each night. After the decision to divorce, I was both *devastated* and *relieved*. I felt *devastated* because I couldn't really believe the marriage was over, but *relieved* that the abuse was over for me. I had failed "big time." I had abandoned my children—they had traded the daily presence of the father who loved them for weekend visits—and I also lost my sense of personal confidence. I believed before that I could do anything, achieve anything and solve any problem, but that confidence was now gone. I did not fully recover that confidence until after my second divorce, almost forty years later.

During my second marriage, thankfully, I did find a personal relationship with God. During our divorce, I went through a period of depression, which I did not perceive as such, for over a year—I thought I was just tired. Then I recognized that, even when I had slept seven or eight hours several days in a row, I was still tired. I realized my "tiredness" was not tiredness but depression. When I finally came to accept my depression, I received some helpful and comforting counsel from God:

"My son, you do well to see your depression. It is the end of life as you knew it, and you do not wish to start again. But you must —and you are— and you shall do more. Be encouraged by this and enjoy your day, My beloved son." (Thursday, September 29, 2005, a.m.)

After I had come to terms with my depression, I took an herbal anti-depressant—St. John's Wort—for six months, until I was no longer depressed. I was *very disappointed* that we couldn't salvage our thirty-six-year marriage but again *relieved* that the abuse was over for me. I had believed we would see our marriage restored (Joel 2:25) and might even have a healing ministry to other couples in hopeless situations like ours.

Divorce is a very serious and, unfortunately, sometimes necessary, step to take in order for you to maintain your love for yourself. Harville Hendrix is a former Baptist Pastor who wrote *Getting the Love You Want* in an effort to discover the causes of divorce—initially his own very painful divorce, so as to never again go through such an experience. His findings are insightful. He says,

> You fell in love because [you] had your partner confused with your parents! . . . [You] had finally found the ideal candidate to make up for the psychological and emotional damage you experienced in childhood (14). . . . [You were] attempting to return to the scene of your original frustration so that you could resolve your unfinished business [from childhood] (36). . . . [My clients] react to their partners as if they were carbon copies of their parents (75).

He also believes if you divorce *before* resolving your "unfinished business from childhood," you'll *again* make a similar choice if you remarry. I believe we try to restore or match the conditions of our childhood home when marrying. If we came from an unhappy home, we unconsciously look for a mate who will help us replicate those conditions, as Hendrix discusses. Alternatively, if our home was a *happy* one, then I believe that's the situation we'll try to duplicate with our spousal choice![10]

One final ironic comment on divorce: in Switzerland, the home country of Calvinism, people are now getting divorced *in church*! Kesterton, in one of his "Social Studies" tidbits, quotes Ruedi Reich, president of the Zurich Reform Church, as saying "Going through a ceremony [of divorce in church] like this is a way of showing God that the marriage is over."

Abortion

And what about abortion? How do the two love commandments apply to the foetus? Life begins at *conception* and *not at birth*, as ultrasound photos reveal. In an abortion, the foetus is murdered; however, the sin of abortion, like all sins, will be forgiven if repented of.

ABORTION

The main argument in favour of abortion is that as long as the child is in the woman's body, he/she is a part of the woman's body—a body with which she is free to do as she pleases, since it is *her* body! The child has no existence independent of its mother! And since women have the law on their side in most, if not all, jurisdictions on this topic, there is unlikely to be any legal argument that that the anti-abortion/pro-life side can raise. I'll use two arguments with respect to abortion as murder, the first by analogy and the second from the Bible.

[10] In chapter 6 I trace how my personal development led to my marital choices and to my painful divorces in the sections entitled "The Experience of a Journey of Recovery" and "A Personal Testimony."

The Argument by Analogy

A newborn child is dependent on its parents for its existence probably until adolescence. That being the case, why aren't the parents free to murder the child as long as it is so dependent on them, as long as he/she has no independent existence? If it's a valid argument when the child is dependent on its mother for its existence, why not for as long as it's still dependent on its parents for its existence? In the Roman times of Jesus day, it was apparently legal for parents to abandon unwanted children and leave them to die by the roadside—a Roman era precursor to abortion. If they're murdered before the age of reason, you could argue that you're doing them a favour, not only by sparing them the hardships of life, but also by guaranteeing them a place in heaven.

Most people will recoil in horror from such an argument. To most people, it is monstrous to kill a living person. But remember, the foetus, like the dependent child, is a living being. If it's okay to deliberately kill the one—the foetus—it seems to me it's not such a big stretch to think it's okay to murder the other—the dependent child.

The Argument from the Bible

Psalm 139 shows clearly that the conceived but unborn child is considered a person by God. Verses 14–16 state it best (the "you" in these verses refers to God, the "I" is King David, a representative human being): "I praise you because I am fearfully and wonderfully made. . . . My frame was not hidden from you when I was made in the secret place. When I was woven together in the depths of the earth, your eyes saw my unformed body. All the days ordained for me were written in your book before one of them came to be." See also Jeremiah 1:5. Since these verses contradict no others, as with all other scriptures, they are true!

To wreck vengeance on the inconvenient foetus is contrary to God's command, as Deuteronomy 32:35 and Romans 12:19 tell us. In the New Testament, Jesus made it even more stringent, since He tells us we are to "love our enemies" in Matthew 5:38–48 and Luke 10:25–28, which applies even to the inconvenient foetus. And in Genesis 9:5b, God says, "And from each man [and woman], too, I will demand an accounting for the life [that is taken] of his fellow man [human being, including the foetus]."

Capital Punishment

I believe that both abortion and capital punishment are murder! God protected the first murderer, Cain (Genesis 4:1–16), God also says vengeance belongs to Him (Deuteronomy 32:35, Romans 12:19), and Jesus commuted the death sentence of the woman caught in adultery—perhaps a capital punishment crime in those days—encouraging her instead to lead a repentant life (John 8:1–11). God instituted capital punishment for some sins during the Exodus from Egypt (Exodus 21:12–22:20) for two reasons: 1. those who sinned would be rebelling against the leading of God the Holy Spirit, who was visibly present with them throughout their journey across the desert (Exodus 13:21–22, 14:19–25, 40:34–38; Numbers 9:15–23; Deuteronomy 1:32–33), and 2. the Israelite community, living in close proximity to each other, were very susceptible to the infectious influence of sinful examples, as the golden calf incident (Exodus 32), only one of many incidents, illustrates. God also instituted capital punishment for murder and other serious sins in Israel (Deuteronomy 18-25).

CAPITAL PUNISHMENT

In Genesis 9:5–6, God says, "And from each man, too, I will demand an accounting for the life of his fellow man. Whoever sheds the blood of man, by man shall his blood be shed; for in the image of God has God made man.'" This means we are not to take another's life, but if we do, we enter a lifestyle of violence where our own life may be forfeit as well. During the Exodus period, the time of "an eye for an eye and a tooth for a tooth," anyone who took the life of another human being were themselves to be put to death (Leviticus 24:17–22).

In Numbers 35:9–34, Deuteronomy 19:4–13, and Joshua 20:1–9, as the Israelites were preparing to take over the Canaanite land promised to them, they were told by God to deal with murder in the following ways (cf. Exodus 21:12–14):

1. For the unintentional killing of a person, the accidental murderer could take refuge in a designated "city of refuge" and he would be safe there if he remained until the death of the current high priest. However, if he left the city of refuge prior to the death of the high priest, the "avenger of blood" could kill him with impunity.
2. If the killing was intentional, the deliberate murderer was himself to be killed, again by the "avenger of blood," with impunity, wherever the murderer was.

The "avenger of blood" was a member of the extended family of the murder victim. He was a "blood" relative, not an agent of the victim's tribe or of the nation of Israel. Murder was common enough in those times that such a system was essential to maintaining civil order.

In the New Testament (Matthew 5:38–48, Luke 10:25-28), Jesus said we are to "love our enemies." Under this scenario, an "avenger of blood" would no longer seek "an eye for an eye, and a tooth for a tooth." In other words, he would no longer seek to end the life of the murderer but would rather "love" him. And it's not only in the New Testament, but also in the Old Testament, that we are counselled to be merciful to our enemies. In Proverbs 24:29 we are told not to repay "an eye for an eye, and a tooth for a tooth." Even more strongly, Proverbs 25:21–22, which is cited in Romans 12:21–22, tells us to "love our enemies" by blessing them.

How to truly love a violent offender is explained in the introduction to chapter 5.

Choosing Sin or Holiness

Temptation is what leads to sin—or to holiness.

James explains it most succinctly:

> When tempted, no one should say "God is tempting me." For God cannot be tempted by evil, nor does he tempt anyone; but each one is tempted when, by his own evil desire, he is dragged away and enticed. Then, after desire has conceived, it gives birth to sin; and sin, when it is full-grown, gives birth to [spiritual] death (James 1:13–15).

Not only are we responsible for succumbing to temptations, Jesus also names some of the character flaw reasons why we succumb to temptation: "[Jesus said] from within, out of men's [people's] hearts, come evil thoughts, sexual immorality, theft, murder, adultery, greed, malice, deceit, lewdness, envy, slander, arrogance and folly" (Mark 7:21). Jesus, our model, never succumbed to temptation: "[Jesus was] tempted in every way, just as we are – yet was without sin" (Hebrews 4:15). Jesus' reliance on God the Holy Spirit enabled Him to withstand all temptations.

If you call on Him, God the Holy Spirit "will not let you be tempted beyond what you can bear. But when you are tempted, he will also provide a way out so that you can stand up under it" (1 Corinthians 10:13b). In other words, if we ask God's help, we too can resist temptation.

I've applied the model, depicted here, to a number of biblical examples.

1. **Human Condition:** We have a variety of *needs and wants*: physical, emotional, economic, social, maturational, and spiritual.
2. **Temptation:** The *obstacles* we encounter sometimes frustrate our desires to satisfy our wants and needs.

3. **Choice:** We can react to frustration either *lovingly* or *sinfully*.
4. **Consequences:** Loving choices lead to *peace and eternal life*; serious sinful choices lead to *turmoil* and, if unrepented, *eternal death in hell.*

Adam, the First Man

1. **Need**: Adam wanted to be equal to God in wisdom (Genesis 3:5).
2. **Temptation**: Adam was offered fruit from the Tree of the Knowledge of Good and Evil by Eve (Genesis 3:3, 6).
3. **Choice**: Adam ate the fruit and learned of evil (Genesis 3:6–7).
4. **Consequence**: Adam did not repent, but rather, blamed Eve and God for his choice and, as a result, Adam and Eve and their descendents lost their earthly paradise, the Garden of Eden, forever (Genesis 3:11–19).

Cain, the First Son of Adam and Eve

1. **Need**: Cain wanted God's esteem (Genesis 4:3–5).
2. **Temptation**: Cain expected to get as favourable a reaction to his offering as his brother Abel did, but that expectation was frustrated by God's reaction to their offerings: favourable to Abel's but not to Cain's, a situation to which Cain reacted in anger (Genesis 4:3–5).
3. **Choice**: Cain chose sin and murdered Abel (Genesis 4:6–8).
4. **Consequence**: Cain lied to God about what he'd done and suffered because of his unrepented sin for the rest of his life (Genesis 4:9–16).

David, the Second King of Israel

1. **Need**: King David wanted to have sex with Bathsheba (2 Samuel 11:2).
2. **Temptation**: David's desire was for Bathsheba, but there was an obstacle—she was Uriah's wife (2 Samuel 11:2–3). Uriah was one of the "mighty men" in King David's army (2 Samuel 23:39, 1 Chronicles 11:41).
3. **Choice**: David chose sin. He had sex with Bathsheba, who became pregnant (2 Samuel 11:4–5), and then, unable to get her husband Uriah to sleep with her and so conceal his adultery, David had him killed (2 Samuel 11:6–21).
4. **Consequence**: The prophet Nathan told David that his household would suffer calamitously for his sin, which it did (2 Samuel 12:15–20:26), but David admitted his sin and repented, so he was restored (2 Samuel 11:26–12:14; Psalm 51).

Job, a Hebrew Patriarch Who Lived More than 1000 Years Before Christ Was Born

1. **Need**: Job wanted his skin to be normal/healed (Job 2:1–8).
2. **Temptation**: Job's desire was to be healed (Job 2:7–8) or to die (Job 2:9, 3:1–26); he could have died by cursing God.
3. **Choice**: Job made the very difficult but holy choice and avoided sin (Job 2:10).
4. **Consequence**: Job's health and prosperity were restored (Job 42:7–17).

Satan, an Angel Who Went Bad

1. **Need**: Satan desired to be equal in power and majesty to God (Isaiah 14:12–14).
2. **Temptation**: He was a mighty angel who wanted the recognition of godhood instead of being content with recognition as one of the mightiest of angels (Isaiah 14:12–14; Ezekiel 28:12–14).
3. **Choice**: Satan made the proud sinful choice (Isaiah 14:13–14; Ezekiel 28:15).
4. **Consequence**: He was banished from heaven to eternal suffering in hell (Isaiah 14:15, Ezekiel 28:16–19, Luke 10:18, Revelation 12:7–9, 20:10).

The Consequences of Sin

So, in general, what happens after you sin? Ezekiel 18, which expands upon Deuteronomy 24:16, makes it most clear. Verse 20 states: "The soul who sins is the one who will die." Now, we know that all human life ends—we die—so what is the death this passage is referring to? It means your soul/spirit dies. Most simply stated, here on earth you've cut off your relationship with God and, when you die physically, you'll go to hell—spiritual death—and not to heaven. And since everyone sins (Romans 3:23), you'd think that heaven would be empty and hell would be "standing room only." However, if you think that, thank God, you're wrong, as Ezekiel 18:21 explains: "But if a wicked man turns away from all the sins he has committed and keeps all my decrees and does what is just and right [i.e., repents], he will surely live; he will not die." For instance, Psalm 51 shows King David's repentance over his adultery with Bathsheba.

Prior to Christ the Messiah's atoning death, all the repentant dead were not in eternal hell, but rather, in a Limbo section of hell, awaiting redemption (Luke 16:22–26). Yom Kippur, the Jewish Day of Atonement, is the holiest of their holy days. On that day, up until the destruction of the second Temple, atonement was made for the sins of the citizens of Israel through the sacrifice of the scapegoat on whose head the sins of the nation were symbolically laid (see Leviticus 16, especially verses 10 and 21–22). I say "symbolically" because, as Hebrews 10:4 explains, animal sacrifice cannot literally atone for human sin. True atonement requires a perfect *human* sacrifice, which was accomplished by the crucifixion of the Messiah, Jesus the Christ. This is explained in Isaiah 52:13–53:12; the opening up of hell and freeing of the dead from their Limbo in hell to go to heaven occurred after the death of Jesus as described in Matthew 27:50–53. This topic is more fully dealt with in chapter 4.

Suffering

What are the causes of suffering? As illustrated by the example of Job above and John 9:1–3 (the man born blind), suffering is not always a consequence of sin. So, then, why else do people suffer? Again, as previous examples illustrate, sin *can* be a cause of suffering. But it's not the only reason. Let's try to understand the causes of suffering.

1. **Disobedience to God's Commands (Sin)** – Exodus 15:26, Deuteronomy 28:15–68, Psalm 107:17–18, John 5:13–14.

We know that the 613 commands boil down to two: to love God and to love—do what's best for—ourselves and others. If we want to do what's best for ourselves, we'll follow Jesus the man's prescription for living a full life as given in Luke 2:52. We'll grow in wisdom, or mentally; stature, or physically; in favour with God, or spiritually; and people, or socially. This is similar to the prescription for living implied in Abraham Maslow's Hierarchy of Needs. In 2 Thessalonians 3:10 Paul also reminds us of our need to work.

If we do these things, we won't abuse ourselves with addictive substances (drugs, alcohol, cigarettes, etc.) or food (compulsive eating, binging/purging, etc.) and we'll keep physically fit. We won't isolate but will be socially active. We'll keep learning and keep our minds growing. We'll be productive members of society—law-abiding and generating income. We'll have an active relationship with God. And we'll reap the benefits of that lifestyle.

If we do what's best for others, we won't, among other things, abuse our world by over-fishing or over-harvesting our other resources or polluting our environment.

2. **Providence** – Psalm 73; Ecclesiastes 7:15, 8:14; Jeremiah 12:1; John 9:1–3.

Sometimes we cannot or do not understand why we suffer and others, who seem less deserving, are blessed.

3. **Satan** – Job 1:6-2:10, Luke 4:1–13, 22:31–62.

Sometimes God allows the devil to torment us.

4. **Injustice Here on Earth** – Genesis 39:1–20, Jeremiah 19:10–20:8, Luke 13:1–4.

Sometimes what happens to us here on Earth just doesn't seem fair; our suffering seems to have no redeeming quality. But sometimes, the experience of your suffering may allow you to bring comfort to those going through a similar experience (2 Corinthians 1:3–5, Hebrews 2:18). Or perhaps your suffering will strengthen your faith (Psalm 119:67, 71; 2 Corinthians 12:7–10; Hebrews 12:1–13). Many people's faith in God has been strengthened during their time of suffering. One example that comes to mind is Joni Eareckson Tada, who relates in *Joni* how she developed a wonderful faith and a blessed ministry through a tragic accident.

5. **Persecution for Your Faith** – Matthew 5:11–12; Acts 5:12–42; 2 Timothy 3:10–13; 1 Peter 4:16, 19.

To practice your faith can lead to persecution or death in some parts of the world and ridicule or shame in others.

So, as we can see, there are many reasons for suffering, only some of which are of our own doing. In my times of suffering, none of which I appreciated at the time I was going through the suffering, I frequently reminded myself of the promise of Romans 8:28—that God would bring good out of my suffering at some point.

Death

It is popularly said, "The only sure thing in life is death and taxes," but the truth is the only one that's sure is death. Hebrews 9:27 tells us that we live once, die, and then face the judgment of God. There's no second chance through reincarnation or an experience like that of the Phil Connors character (played by Bill Murray) in the film *Groundhog Day*. In the light of eternity, life here on Earth is relatively short, as the Bible reminds us in Psalms 39:5, 144:4; Ecclesiastes 5:18; and James 4:14.

Regarding death, there is no record of the deaths of two people: Enoch (Genesis 5:24, Hebrews 11:5) and Elijah (2 Kings 2:11–12). Nine people were brought back from the dead: Samuel (1 Samuel 25:1, 28:11–19, although whether he was truly brought back from the dead is controversial), the widow of Zarephath's son (1 Kings 17:17–24), the Shunamite's son (2 Kings 4:8–37), an Israelite corpse (2 Kings 13:21), the Synagogue Ruler's daughter (Matthew 9:18–26), the widow's son (Luke 7:12–17), Lazarus (John 11:1–44), Dorcas (Acts 9:36–42), and Eutychus, who died after falling asleep listening to a sermon (Acts 20:7–12)—but all these people eventually died in the end.

On pages 61–64 of *Beyond Death's Door*, Rawlings describes the generic near-death experience that some people go through. A person loses consciousness and then their spirit/soul views its own physical body from above. After this, the person's spirit/soul goes down a long dark passage toward either a wonderful bright place or a terrible dark place. People revived after such an experience will almost certainly develop a faith in God and change their lives.

Kubler-Ross, in *On Death and Dying*, describes the five stages of the typical actual death experience as follows:

1. *Shock and Denial*. "Not me . . . not death!"

2. *Anger.* "Why me? It's not fair!"
3. *Bargaining.* "If you'll let me live, God, I'll change my ways."
4. *Depression and Grieving.* "It's really happening to me and there's nothing I can do to stop it. I'm so sad. I cry so much."
5. *Acceptance.* "I've only got a little time left—I'd better use it well and prepare for my death."

Heaven and Hell

We all live forever. First, for a relatively few years here on Earth, then, based on the choices we make while here, the rest of eternity in either heaven or hell. Life is a dry run—a dress rehearsal—for eternity. If we live a loving life here on earth, we're preparing for heaven. Alternatively, if we live a selfish, hateful, miserable life—if the life we choose is a "hell on earth"—that's the place we're preparing ourselves for. Hell is reserved for people who are not loving and is described as a horribly painful and terrifying place (Matthew 13:49–50, 25:46; Luke 16:23–24; 2 Thessalonians 1:8–9; Revelation 20:10–15). Heaven is obviously the better alternative to choose, as described in Matthew 11:11; Luke 20:35–36; 1 Corinthians 15:35–55; Philippians 3:20–21; and Revelation 21:3–27.

I believe that we have little, if any, real insight as to what heaven is like. What can we really know about living life forever as a spirit? I believe it will be unimaginably joyous—eternal ecstasy! And I believe the real pain of hell is to forever realize what a fool you've been to choose to be without God for eternity. Be very clear about this: the choice is ours! God does *not condemn* some people to hell and God does *not assign* some people to heaven. A person chooses hell or heaven by the life they have chosen to live here on earth. God, through His Holy Spirit, *encourages* all of us to choose heaven, but He *leaves the choice* of heaven or hell up to us! As God implores us in Ezekiel 33:11, "I take no pleasure in the death of the wicked, but rather that they turn from their ways and live. Turn! Turn from your evil ways! Why will you [choose to] die [live eternally in hell]?" (also see Ezekiel 18:23, 32).

By the way, "heaven" and "sky" are not synonyms, and neither are "hell" and "the earth's core." Heaven is not "up there"—it's a spiritual place, not a physical place—and hell is not "down there"—it's also a spiritual place and not a physical place. As Paul says in 1 Corinthians 15:42–54, we die with physical bodies and are resurrected with spiritual bodies and "they ain't the same thing"! Jesus further tells us, "When the dead rise...they will be like the angels in heaven" (Mark 12:25). Spiritual beings live in spiritual places, whatever that means.

Atheism

God has "set eternity in the hearts of men [people]" (Ecclesiastes 3:11). In other words, all people know intuitively that there is a hereafter, which implies God. I've only known or encountered a small number of Atheists. Those that I've known were Atheists for one of two reasons. One was because they had had an abusive father and the connection with God the *Father* was too strong for them to overcome. The other reason is that they blamed God for some tragedy or disappointment in their lives, believing "If there *really is a God*, He never would have allowed such-and-such to happen." However, the real tragedy is that they will not receive the unconditional love from the only Being who truly loves them unconditionally, instead succumbing to the lies dictated either by their pain or by Satan, who is able to masquerade as an angel of light (2 Corinthians 11:14). Nonetheless, as the Bible assures us, the existence of God and the reality of heaven and hell remain, regardless of our belief or lack of belief in them.

God in the Old and New Testaments

Another apparent conundrum regarding God's nature is that He appears to be cruel in the Old Testament but merciful in the New Testament. Jesus, our Emmanuel, or God with us, seems to manifest a merciful quality absent from God in the Old Testament. As Arends notes in *The Grace of Wrath*, "There are some pretty hard bits in scripture. It is difficult to frame, say, the saga of Sodom and Gomorrah as a love story."

Is this so? Did God have a change of heart between the Old and New Testaments? The answer is No! So then why did God destroy all the peoples of the world except Noah and his family at the time of the Flood, and why did He order the Israelites to destroy most of the Canaanites when they entered the Promised Land?

The "decision tree" concept helps us to understand this. If the decisions that are still open to people are sinful only with *no possibility of repentance* or they have chosen to ignore God speaking to them[11]—in other words, if they are in a situation hopeless because repentance is impossible (Deuteronomy 9:4–5; 32:30, 41)—then God may allow them to be destroyed and sent early from the hell they're living here on earth to their ultimate hell destination (Proverbs 29:1). In the New Testament we have the example of Ananias and Sapphira (Acts 4:34–5:11). On the other hand, if the possibility of repentance still exists, then God is merciful—think of the Ninevites, the ancestors of today's Iraqis, in the Old Testament (Jonah 3:1–10).

There are many other instances of a merciful Old Testament God. For example, God the Father showed tenderness and mercy in how He treated Elijah the prophet when he was in the wilderness (1 Kings 17:1–6, 19:9–18) and in how He treated Naamman the Aramean army commander when He healed him of leprosy (2 Kings 5:1–14). Events where God's mercy occurs may sometimes appear to be chance occurrences, as in the life-saving case of Mordecai and the Persian Jews (Esther 6:1–8:17), but rest assured, there is no "chance" with a "decision tree" God—He always knows *all* the possibilities! It is unfortunate that Elie Wiesel saw his own deliverance from death at the hands of the Nazi as due to "chance" rather than as the result of a possibility preordained by the God who loves him (see Yancey, *Where is God When It Hurts?* 157).

[11] This is a reference to the "Sin against the Holy Spirit," which is fully explained in chapter 4.

Understand this: because God is unchanging, He doesn't change the ground rules. And God doesn't play favourites (Acts 10:34–35); He wants every human being on the face of the Earth to repent and be saved (2 Peter 3:9). The Bible assures us His compassion never fails (Lamentations 3:22–23).

Disasters and God's Call

We do not know why disasters sometimes befall good people. Our ignorance, however, doesn't change God's nature. But when God does speak to you with that still small voice saying, "This is the way; walk in it" (Isaiah 30:21) or specifically gives you a sign, such as a miracle, to draw you to Him and His way and you *ignore* it, then you are rejecting God's call and dooming yourself for eternity. I believe this is what the peoples of the Earth did prior to the Flood and the people of Israel's Promised Land did prior to the Israelites' arrival—they ignored God's call. And that is still the way God operates today! The God of the Old Testament and the God of the New Testament is the same gracious God He has always been and always will be. So if He speaks to *you*, please listen— for *your* sake!

Again, it's important to understand that every time you ignore God speaking to you, it's not a sin against the Holy Spirit."[12] It's a sin against the Holy Spirit *only* if the message He gives is to lead you along the path to salvation—a critical choice point in your life's decision tree—and not if He's merely giving you counsel on helping you lead a loving, or "best," life. In that case, the miserable consequences resulting from your ignoring Him on what's best for you or others will be sufficient!

Disasters

As the section on the causes of suffering indicates, there are risks inherent to living on Planet Earth. That being said, it's also important to understand that the loss of life in *many* of our natural disasters is not a result of a failure on God's part. If

[12] The "Sin against the Holy Spirit" is fully discussed in chapter 4 within the section "The Process of Salvation."

people choose to live in flood plains or hurricane/tornado-prone areas, in the vicinity of an active volcano, or along a significant fault line in the earth's crust, that is not God's doing. Yet rest assured, when the next San Andreas Fault earthquake occurs sometime in the next 30 years (according to California geophysicists cited in an Associated Press story) and numerous lives are lost somewhere between San Francisco and San Diego, many will blame God. The film *San Francisco*, which starred Clark Gable, dramatically depicts the San Francisco earthquake of April 18, 1906. It had a devastating impact on its inhabitants but, according to the film, the survivors were drawn *to* God, and not *away* from Him (Isaiah 26:9).

The "blame God approach" reminds me of the saying attributed to Winston Churchill when he was Prime Minister of Great Britain: "When things are going badly, people blame the Prime Minister, but when things are going well, they sing 'God Save the Queen'." Often people blame God for the disasters that befall them, but attribute their success to their own skill or uniquely deserved good fortune.

Final Comments on the God of the Bible

I observe that evangelical churches frequently speak against the "social ills" of our day. Jesus *never* did, even though social conditions were far worse in His day. Why is that? I believe it's because a focus on social conditions would have diverted attention from *what is central to God's message to us here on earth.* His priority was that we understand the need to repent of our sins—specifically character sins of commission and omission, salvation by grace, and the need to live a life of love toward God, oneself, and others. The twelve steps groups avoid such distractions by observing their Tradition Ten, which states "[The twelve step groups have] no opinion on outside issues, hence [our] name ought never be drawn into public controversy" (AA, 564). I believe the adoption of a similar guideline by Evangelical Christian Churches would do much to enhance the spread of the Gospel message. These "outside issues" are the *Devil's distractions*.

In fact, rather than the negative focus on "outside issues," or *dis*-tractions, evangelical churches would do better to see them as *at*-tractions, or outreach links, as the twelve steppers do. For instance, the fourth chapter of the AA "Big Book" is written to agnostics and atheists, and Al-Anon has a pamphlet welcoming gays and lesbians. The reason why evangelicals typically *don't* do this kind of outreach is illustrated by the remarks of an evangelical acquaintance. His reaction to the appearance of a "street person" at his church the prior Sunday *looking for salvation* was, "He should have cleaned himself up first."

We're all sinners, some saved by grace. The requirement for a person going to church should not be "I've got to clean myself up first," but rather, "Just as I am"!

One positive Christian outreach that I'm aware of is churches setting up booths at "spiritualist fairs," trying to reach the spiritually hungry attendees. But they could do much more to reach the spiritually hungry. As noted in Appendix 1, evangelical churches often have signs saying "Sinners welcome," so they should *welcome* fornicating heterosexuals, homosexuals, those who cheat on their taxes and on their spouses, and all other sinners. The only sinners who should be *excluded* are those who *promote a sinful lifestyle within the church*! To classify a sin such as homosexual sex as a greater sin than the sins common among evangelicals is the sin of *pride*, as demonstrated in the parable of the Pharisee and the Tax Collector (Luke 18:9–14)! All sin is sin—*there are no okay sins*—all sin is *not okay*! For an evangelical to think, "God, I thank you that I am not like [these sinful] other men" (Luke 18:11) is to miss that point completely (Jeremiah 32:27, John 3:16)!

3 GOD THE HOLY SPIRIT

Contents

Develop Perspective on God the Holy Spirit

Before reading this chapter, first bring your *own* perspective to the topic of "God the Holy Spirit" by answering the following questions:

1. What are the main roles of God the Holy Spirit here on Earth?
2. Are there any differences in His roles with the saved and the unsaved?
3. What is the Sin against the Holy Spirit? Is it unforgivable? Why or why not?
4. What role, if any, did the Holy Spirit have in the writing of the Bible?
5. What role does the Holy Spirit have in your life?
6. Are you troubled with excess anger or resentment? If yes, how do you think you could deal with it so you could be rid of it for good? How could God help you in dealing with your anger and resentment?
7. Has anything you've been told about God the Holy Spirit in church confused you or turned you off? Explain. (e.g., He's God the Father's Spirit, Jesus' Ghost, or not even a real separate spiritual person.)

Overview of the Chapter

So, as you have seen, God the Father created the physical world and, as you will see, God the Son—Jesus the Messiah or Christ—made possible salvation by grace through His atoning sacrifice. However, God the Holy Spirit is the member of the Trinity who is involved with the earth and us its inhabitants on an ongoing basis.

- God the Holy Spirit's role as Counsellor and five of His other characteristics are discussed. The Holy Spirit led the Hebrews through the Sinai desert to the Promised Land (Hebrews 3:7–11) and, if we listen to that "still small voice" (Isaiah 30:21), He will lead us today.
- The three main relationships with God the Holy Spirit are described. Examples of the Holy Spirit's leading are given, both biblical and personal; these reveal the development of intimacy in a relationship with God.

Introduction

The Greek word *pneuma*, meaning 'breath' or 'breeze' is used to refer to the Holy Spirit, also called the Spirit of God. So when 2 Timothy 3:16 says that all Scripture is "God-breathed," it means that the Scripture writer was literally inspired by God the Holy Spirit to write what he wrote. God the Holy Spirit also calls people to ministry (e.g., in Acts 13:2 the church at Antioch was called to "set aside" Saul/Paul and Barnabas for ministry). In the King James Bible translation, the term used for Holy Spirit is "Holy Ghost," the term also used in the Apostles' Creed translation given in chapter 1.

Characteristics of God the Holy Spirit

1. Involved in Creation

After God created the heavens and the earth, the Spirit of God hovered over the waters and was involved with the creation from that point on (Genesis 1:1–2).

2. Counsellor

Jesus refers to the Holy Spirit as our Counsellor (John 14:26, 15:26). The Holy Spirit will tell the disciples what to say if they are arrested/persecuted (Matthew 10:17–20). The Holy Spirit will convict and counsel the people of the world about sin and righteousness and teach the disciples about God the Son (John 16:7–15). The Holy Spirit guided the choices of where the apostles went to minister (Acts 16:6–10). Isaiah 30:21 says, "Whether you turn to the right or to the left, your ears will hear a voice behind you, saying, 'This is the way, walk in it.'" This is how the Holy Spirit counsels all people and *this is how God has always interacted with humankind.* Proverbs 3:5–6 promises: "Trust in the Lord with all your heart and lean not on your own understanding; in all your ways acknowledge him, and he will make your paths straight."

Other ways that God provides counsel

Besides the "still small voice" of the Holy Spirit, there are several other ways that God communicates with us.

SCRIPTURE

The counsel you follow should never be in disagreement with what the Bible says on the subject. Psalm 19:7–9 assures us that "The law of the Lord is perfect, reviving the soul. The statutes of the Lord are trustworthy, making wise the simple. The precepts of the Lord are right, giving joy to the heart. . . . The ordinances of the Lord are sure and altogether righteous." In my many readings of Scripture, I felt God "quicken" or nudge my spirit whenever He had a message from Scripture for me. Different passages were drawn to my attention at different times, depending upon what counsel God was seeking to impart to me. If you read the Bible, He'll do the same for you.

COMMON SENSE

Does your intuition or the counsel you've received from others make sense; is it reasonable? We may not always understand His purpose, but God is never unreasonable. Proverbs 2:6 tells us, "For the Lord gives wisdom, and from his mouth comes knowledge and understanding." Paul reminds us in 1 Corinthians 14 that "God is not a God of disorder," (33) and, "everything should be done in a fitting and orderly way" (40).

PERSONAL

If someone tells you they have a message from God for you, it should be a confirmation of something God has already told you and not some brand new revelation. We do not need people to mediate our relationship with God *unless we are refusing to listen* to God, in which case an intermediary may be necessary. For instance, Balaam the prophet needed a donkey (Numbers 22:21–35), Eli the priest needed Samuel (1 Samuel 2:22–3:21), and David the king needed Nathan (2 Samuel 11:2–4 and 12:1–13) in order to get the message God had for them.

CIRCUMSTANCES

Are circumstances supportive? If it is really the will of God, no insurmountable obstacle will be put in your path. Acts 16:7 illustrates an insurmountable obstacle: "When they [Paul and his travelling companions] came to the border of Mysia, they tried to enter Bithynia, but the Spirit of Jesus would not allow them to." Alternatively, if circumstances are dictating that you ought to change your current life direction, you would be wise to do so. My favourite is the first of the twelve steps of AA: "We admitted we were powerless over alcohol [or any other obstacle to our living a loving life]–that that our lives had become *unmanageable*" (AA, 59, emphasis added).

ONE LAST CAVEAT ON GOD'S COUNSEL

A wise Christian teacher, Danny Paul, gave me this bit of wisdom on the topic many years ago when I was new to the faith. His comment was that "With the Lord, there are many more *yellow* lights than either red or green." In other words, most of the time, you will *not* get clear direction from God on a possible course of action. So you start out in faith on your course of action with your "yellow light" and see whether future circumstances turn the light green or red. My writing of this book is an example of one of God's "yellow lights."

3. Comforter/Channel for God's Love

God pours His love into our hearts through the Holy Spirit and fills us with joy and peace (Romans 5:5, 15:13). God brings us comfort when we're troubled, which enables us to do the same for others who are troubled (2 Corinthians 1:3–5). God the Holy Spirit will be with us if we're insulted for our faith (1 Peter 4:14), and 1 Peter 5:7 encourages us with "Cast all your anxiety [worries/ cares] on him [God] because he cares for you."

4. Miracle-Worker

In Matthew 12:22–37, Mark 3:20–30, and Luke 11:14–20, Jesus proclaims that miracles are wrought by God through the Holy Spirit to reveal the hand of God at work in the lives of people. But in these passages, the Pharisees saw how God acted or intervened in human affairs and proudly *denied* that it was from God, which is the unforgivable Sin against the Holy Spirit.[13] To act in ignorance and unbelief is normal or typical (1 Timothy 1:13). In your ignorance, God will be kind and merciful to you because He is trying to lead you to repentance (Romans 2:4). However, when someone consciously rejects the way God is showing them, they have embarked on a path from which there is no return back to the way of God. They know in their hearts that God is speaking to them but they *choose to ignore it.*

5. Multiple Manifestations

- *Dove*: Luke 3:21–22, John 1:29–34.
- *Oil/Water* (anointing substance): Psalm 23:5, 92:10; Isaiah 44:2–3; Joel 2:28–29; John 7:37–39; Acts 2:17–18; 1 John 2:20, 27.

[13] This topic will be fully explained in the section "The Process of Salvation" in chapter 4.

- *Wind*: John 3:8; Acts 2:2, 4.
- *Fire*: Matthew 3:11, Acts 2:3–4, 1 Thessalonians 5:19, Hebrews 12:28–29.

6. Involved in Salvation and Ministry Empowering

The apostles were saved by Jesus after His resurrection when He breathed on them and said, "Receive the Holy Spirit" (John 20:22; cf. 7:39; Ezekiel 11:19; Acts 5:32, Titus 3:4–7). Psalm 14:2 reminds us that the Lord "looks down from Heaven" and knows those who are seeking God.

The Apostles received the Inspiration of the Holy Spirit to empower them for ministry as described in Acts 1:1–9 and 2:1–41. However, the Holy Spirit empowering for ministry was also given to leaders in the Old Testament. For example:

- *Moses and the 70 elders*: Numbers 11:10–17, 24–30.
- *Joshua*: Numbers 27:12–23, Deuteronomy 34:1–9.
- *Samson*: Judges 13:1–5, 24–25; 14:1–16:30.
- *Saul,* the first king of Israel: 1 Samuel 10:1, 9–13, 21–24.
- *Jeremiah* the prophet: Jeremiah 1:1–10, 17–19; 26:1–7; 28:1–17; 36:1–3; cf. 2 Peter 1:20–21.
- *Bezalel and Oholiab,* who constructed the physical requirements for God-worship (the Tabernacle) during the Exodus from Egypt, also received Holy Spirit empowering: Exodus 31:1–11; 35:30–36:5.

My favourite example, though, is the reluctant Gideon, who became one of Israel's "judges," or leaders, as described in Judges chapters 6–8. Before accepting God's commission as Israel's leader, Gideon asked for two "fleece-test" proofs that it was really God who was speaking to him: the first that a fleece on the ground be made wet one night and the second that it be made dry the next night (6:36–40). Then God enabled him to defeat a vast Midianite army with only 300 men—120,000 of the enemy's soliders were killed in battle (7:1–8:21)—after which Gideon was made leader of Israel (8:22–26).

Relationship: Holy Spirit to Humankind

1. To guide all humankind in choosing the godly path

The "still small voice" of God (Isaiah 30:21), or conscience, is the primary way God *always* speaks to people to lead them to Him and away from evil. This is how God spoke to Samuel when He told him His prophecy for Eli because of the evil in Eli's ministry (1 Samuel 3:1–4:20) and to Elijah after he fled in fear from the evil Jezebel (1 Kings 19:1–18). Since Satan can also speak to people, it's important to know that the message you're getting is really from God. The acid test is that the guidance you receive is loving—what's *best* for you or others. If the counsel you receive is to do wrong, to behave sinfully or to not do what's best, it's *not* from God (James 1:13–15). Also, God may convict you of sinful behaviour—an attack of conscience—but He'll never *condemn* you for it (John 8:9–11, Romans 8:1, 2 Corinthians 3:9), which would be an attack on your value as a child of God and as a human being.

2. To confirm your relationship and provide ongoing counsel

God the Holy Spirit indwells you once you have made a commitment to God in order to confirm the relationship that you have established with Him. Once you have this relationship with God, the Holy Spirit inhabits you constantly and is available to help with all of your choices (John 3:3–8; 14:16–17, 26), whereas prior to salvation, God the Holy Spirit would speak to you at critical choice points (Isaiah 30:21) to guide you toward the path to God, including avoiding evil choices. God the Holy Spirit has spoken to me many times since my salvation to guide me toward more loving choices. Appendix 1 shows a fairly *typical* example of the counsel I've received, and the following are some of my more *noteworthy* examples.

Justice from my Manager. Approximately eight years after my salvation experience, when I was in my late 40s, my manager at the large multi-national company where I worked opted for retirement because of an excellent financial package offered to him by the company. When he retired, I would become manager. The only problem was that *he didn't want to retire*, as his then administrative person told me, so he looked for ways to show that I wasn't up to the job in hopes of necessitating his being called back to continue in the job as an external consultant after retirement. For instance, he reviewed one of my trip expense reports "with a fine toothed comb" to discover errors and found one: I had failed to *claim* a travel expense for which I was entitled and had included a receipt. When I found out what he was doing, I became furious and, after a weekend of reflection, planned to confront his boss with the facts of the situation. But before I did that, I thought I'd run it by God first, even though I *knew* I was right.

God impressed upon me to read Titus chapter two. When I got to verse 9, the message I got was to "keep my mouth shut." This really upset me—so much so that I started reminding God of other scriptures that supported *my* position. However, I knew that I'd had my answer from God, like it or not, so I kept my mouth shut. And of course, as always, God's answer was best.

I got the manager's job when the manager retired, without him coming back as a consultant to oversee me or my lousing up any relationships. My now ex-manager also found the consulting job he was looking for, but with another company.

My own consulting business. Even prior to becoming manager, I had had the "dream" of having my own consulting business. Then, not long after becoming manager, I attended a career and values seminar, "Blessing-White's Managing Personal Growth," where I turned my dream into a goal. But I was unclear on how to achieve my goal. Then one day, after a year or so as manager, I was having lunch in the company cafeteria with a colleague from another location. During lunch, he mentioned that he was starting his own consulting business with support from the company; they were going to give him a contract for consulting work. I then started looking for an opportunity to do the same thing at my location. Soon, I became impatient, and considered quitting to start my own consultancy. However, family obligations and the fact that I knew this was *not* the will of God kept me from acting precipitously.

Not long after, a company reorganization presented the opportunity that I had been looking for. I was given an enhanced pension—for which I had not asked—and a one-year consulting contract, which was renewed for a second year. I continued to get consulting assignments from the company for most of the fourteen years I had the consulting business, and *all* of the other clients I had during my consulting business years were the result of relationships established when I was employed by my former company. Being in business for myself instead of working for a public company gave me lots of discretionary time; that time was vital for me to have available in order to receive the healing that God knew I needed. Waiting on God's timing was a wise thing for me to do!

Compulsiveness regarding time. I used to be very compulsive regarding time. I was fearful of being late for work or missing business flights or work project deadlines, and so I sometimes relied on two alarm clocks to awaken me, one electrical and the other mechanical. Almost ten years after being saved, I had a dream one night. In that dream, I was staying in a strange house and, when I woke up, I got ready and left to attend a meeting somewhere without taking any of the things I needed to bring to the meeting. Shortly after I'd left, I realized that I had left the things that I needed to bring to the meeting, which included my Bible, in the house. So I turned around to go back to the house to get them and saw that all the houses around me looked exactly the same—I didn't know which one I had been staying in. Now I knew I was going to be *late* for the meeting, so I panicked, which woke me up.

God then spoke to me in His still small voice about my time compulsiveness and told me from then on I did not need to worry anymore about being on time or using alarm clocks—He would *always* wake me up on time. And since then, I have *never* used alarm clocks and God has *always* awakened me on time without exception!

Early on in this new arrangement of God waking me up, though, I thought God had let me down. I was supposed to meet an old friend and his wife for dinner at Hotel A in downtown Montreal at 6 p.m. After a day of working for the large multinational company, I'd lain down for a nap at my hotel, Hotel B, which was close by, and didn't wake up till 6 p.m. I quickly got ready, all the while reminding God of His promise and feeling "let down." When I got to Hotel A between 6:10 and 6:15 p.m., my friend was there, but he informed me that his wife was delayed and wouldn't be there until 6:30 p.m. So I got to see that while I thought I knew I was late, God knew I wasn't. Similar incidents have happened to me many times over the years, *always* in the same way: I thought I knew what "on time" was, but God really knew. Today, I know I'm never late if I follow God's prompting.

Communion with God

For the first eleven or so years after my salvation experience I was, in religious terms, a kind of Pharisee, and in healing/recovery terms, a "dry drunk." In my head, I knew that God loved me (John 3:16), but I did not know it in my heart. Soon after going into my own consulting business, I attended a one-day seminar called "Communion with God," taught by Mark Virkler. The seminar showed people how to quiet themselves and listen for God's "still small voice." While many people at the seminar heard God's voice that day, I did not, because I was not able to quiet my mind enough to eliminate my own incessant thinking (Psalm 46:10), nor was I successful the next day, although I did see an image of a scene from Psalm 23: a quiet meadow beside still waters. On the third day, however, I heard a voice—had a thought—in my head that I knew was not my own, but God's. Since then, I listen for God's voice every day. Over the years, I have learned in my *heart* that God loves *me*! That heart knowledge started me on the *road of love*, which is:

1. God loves you unconditionally.
2. You come to believe in your heart that God loves you unconditionally just as you are.[14]
3. You love God back because you know He loved you first (1 John 4:19). How can you not love the God who loves you just as you are, imperfections, faults and all?
4. You start to love yourself unconditionally, since you can't be arrogant enough to set your standards higher than God's (Matthew 22:35–39). If God can love you unconditionally, then surely you can love yourself that way too.
5. As you grow in unconditional love for yourself, you are enabled to love others the same way (Matthew 22:35–39). Remember, you can't give away what you do not have.
6. You love others unconditionally.

That seminar was truly the beginning of my deep healing. My healing involved many counselling sessions and twelve step recovery meetings as well as much deep reflection on my part about my life and my past. I also received healing from three of the perhaps dozen churches that I visited after my salvation experience. Two, pastored by Jim Cantelon and Mark Hazzard, were PAOC. The third was the Toronto Airport Vineyard, now TACF, pastored by John Arnott. However, be clear on this: God has many other approaches to healing that he can use, as the testimony of Charles Stanley in Moody monthly (one among many) illustrates. Pastor Stanley received healing from God through the requested intervention of trusted friends who asked him to envision himself being held in God's loving arms. There

[14] Nouwen's *Life of the Beloved* reinforces this belief.

are numerous ways God can heal you—God is not a "cookie cutter" God!

Dealing with anger and resentments

About six years after the "Communion with God" seminar, I awoke one morning angry over an incident that had happened to me as a child 50 years earlier. It involved an uncle and his friend holding me underwater while swimming. Their intention was, I'm sure, to "have some fun" with the kid. As the kid, however, at the time I was sure they were going to drown me. So I struggled briefly, and then, because they were so much stronger than me, gave up, fully expecting to be drowned. Of course, this was not their intention, and they soon let me go. So as I reflected on my angry thoughts that morning, I remember thinking, "This is nuts to still be resentful over that incident—those guys are both dead now."

God's still small voice then told me that I had many such resentments, and He asked me if I would like Him to show them to me. Surprised, I said Yes. Over the next six months, God showed me over seventy-five individuals, couples or groups toward whom I had resentments. The effect of those resentments was to turn my situational anger into rage, because my reactions to incidents that affected me were not merely reactions to the current situations but fuelled by the anger underlying the unhealed resentments that I still carried around inside of me.

The approach that God showed me to get rid of my resentments and accompanying deep-seated anger was as follows. For each resentment:

1. I returned in my mind to the situation where the resentment first occurred and again tried to feel the feelings of fear, sadness, anger, etc. that I felt when the resentment first arose, and I also looked at how I felt about it now.

2. I did my best to understand my abusers' motives, situations, etc., and then forgave them for being the kind of people who would do that to me. I did *not* forgive them for the abuse itself—that is between them and God, as

the Lord's Prayer points out (Matthew 6:9–15). We ask God to forgive *us* our *wrongdoings* as we forgive *those* who do wrongdoings to us. It's not in *our* power to forgive others their wrongdoings; only God can forgive them their wrongdoings.

3. I released the abusers from my judgement, turned them over to God's judgement, then claimed my freedom from them and felt the emotional release within myself.

After completely dealing with all of my past resentments, which took about two-and-a-half years, my anger became situational and was no longer fuelled by past unforgiven resentments. Now, if unreasonable anger resurfaces or new resentments arise, I again go through the same process to re-obtain my emotional release and freedom. Also, if a deeper healing need surfaces—a healing need not necessarily related to resentments—I use "An Approach to Healing," as described in chapter 6, to facilitate healing.

All deep healing for me has occurred since I was fifty years old. I recall meeting a Psychiatrist when I was in my thirties who told me he used drugs only—not therapy—with clients over fifty. According to an article by Johnson, that's the dominant attitude today among American Psychiatrists for *all* of their clients. I would encourage all mental health professionals to not give up on their clients, even the older ones. The energy required to maintain denial weakens with age!

Parental Resentments

Either when young or in adulthood, children who experienced their parents' divorce, come from a broken or dysfunctional home, come from a home where the death of a parent occurred, never knew a parent because of having been given up for adoption or having been conceived through artificial insemination, and those who had "normal" imperfect parents will typically carry around hurt, unforgiveness, and resentment toward their parents. Here's the letter I wrote in 1998 to my then deceased parents when dealing with my resentments toward them.

Dear Mom and Dad,

1. Situation and Abuse

For years I've held it against you that you did not provide me with a home where I felt safe and secure. Your dysfunctional relationship resulted in bitter verbal fights between you and what felt like conditional love for me—I only felt loved if I was a good boy and not when I messed up.

My feelings as a child were suppressed, since my anger, fear, and sadness were shamed or punished.

As an adult, I'm out of touch with my emotions—I isolate from myself and others and am afraid of intimacy. I'm also usually emotionally unavailable, and abusive when angry. When I return to that time in my mind, I'm really angry—in fact, furious! I've led a sub-optimal existence for almost 60 years because of my upbringing by you two!

2. Understanding and Repentance

I believe you could only show conditional love because that's what you received from your parents. I also believe that you didn't love yourselves unconditionally, so you couldn't love me that way either. As well, I believe you felt threatened by my expressions of feelings. I believe that you did the best you could as parents, but you didn't give me what I needed as a child, and so I've suffered much because of it. Nevertheless, I forgive you for being who you were and I repent of having judged you all these years. I accept your limitations.

3. Release and Claim of Freedom

I release you from my judgement and turn you over to God.

I claim my freedom from the bitter memories that I had of you and our relationship. I feel the emotional release and am free to move on.

After this, I still had one area in dealing with anger that still needed healing. I used to *blame others* for my anger: *they* made me mad! One time I got so angry at another person ("they had made me so angry") that I judged the extremeness of my reaction was more than I could control! I quickly called out to God in my mind and told Him I needed his help to avoid "exploding," calling on His promise in 1 Corinthians 10:13 to not allow me to be tempted beyond what I was able to handle. I was immediately calmed by the peace God gave me. A few hours later at most, I couldn't even understand why I had been angry in the first place.

God showed me, four years after I'd gotten rid of my resentments, that my anger was all mine. And the same was true of all my other emotional reactions—I was responsible for them all. Others didn't make me angry; rather, *I* made myself angry by how I reacted to what they said/did or didn't say/do. My anger at them said, in effect, that I didn't accept them as they were; they would have to behave differently for me to accept them.

EMOTIONAL REACTIONS

The best illustration I've ever heard of the nonsense of blaming others for your emotional reactions was given many years ago by Larry Wilson, then CEO of Wilson Learning. Wilson used a snake to make his point. What follows is a paraphrase of his example.

Wilson stated that many people say, "Snakes frighten me." He then gave an example of three people—I'll call them Sal, Mo, and Chris—presented with the same snake.

1. Sal, who's terrified of snakes, immediately faints.
2. Mo, who's indifferent to snakes, says "Borr-ring."
3. Chris, who really likes snakes, reacts with "Wow—a real-live snake!"

Wilson then pointed out the absurdity of accusing the *same* snake of causing three *different* emotional reactions. It's the person who reacts, not the object or person they react to, that is the cause of the different emotional reactions. Sal's fear, Mo's indifference, and Chris's excitement are a part of their own personal psychological make-up.

> To broaden this lesson and fully make the point, *no one else* makes you happy, sad, angry, fearful, bored, etc. No one determines your emotional reactions but *you*! So if anyone ever says to you, "You make me so angry, I'd like to punch you in the face!" or "You make me so sad, I'm going to cry!" etc., at an appropriate time, you may choose to inform them that *they*, and not you, are *the cause* of their own emotional reactions. And even if you choose not to tell them, at least you'll know the truth!
>
> As a final observation on emotional reactions, Jesus, in pain and dying on the cross, said regarding His executioners, "Father, forgive them, for they do not know what they are doing" (Luke 23:34). Even in this extreme situation, Jesus did not blame His murderers for His pain and suffering. The everyday annoyances that typically occasion our emotional reactions seem very minor by comparison!

Not listening to God's Counsel

Only once did I fail to heed God's counsel. I don't remember exactly what it was, but it had something to do with handling a family matter. God suggested one course of action but I chose to do it my way, which was, in my mind, not much different than God's suggestion. I couldn't have been more wrong. I managed to needlessly alienate my entire family for a considerable period of time by my choice. Since then, I have *never* ignored God's counsel. Most of the time, I proceed through life without the explicit counsel of God. But whenever I get it, I never ignore it—that one experience was enough! The verses of Isaiah 50:10–11 are particularly pointed regarding God's counsel: "Who among you fears the Lord and obeys the word of his servant? Let him who walks in the dark, who has no light, trust in the name of the Lord and rely on his God." This is verse 10, exhorting us to seek counsel from God when unsure of how to deal with an important matter. And verse 11 explains the consequence of trusting one's own counsel instead of God's: "But now, all you who light fires and provide yourselves with flaming torches, go, walk in the light of your fires and of the torches you have set ablaze [i.e., those who follow their own counsel and ignore God's, as I did]. This is what you shall receive from my hand: You will lie down in torment." As noted above, I created "torment" for myself for a considerable period of time.

3. To empower people to do the work of God

In both the Old and New Testaments, God the Holy Spirit inspires people called to do God's work and empowers them to do it. In the last part of the previous section on the Characteristics of the Holy Spirit, examples were given of empowered Old Testament disciples and of the Twelve Apostles ministry. However, many *individual* New Testament disciples were also empowered by the Holy Spirit.

PETER

- in the healing of the crippled beggar (Acts 3:1–10).
- in dealing with Ananias and Sapphira (Acts 5:1–11).
- in dealing with Simon the Sorcerer (Acts 8:9–25).
- in his dream and subsequent dealing with Cornelius and the other Gentile believers (Acts 10:1–48).
- in his miraculous escape from prison (Acts 12:1–19).

PHILLIP

- in his ministry to the Ethiopian Treasurer (Acts 4:26–40).
- in his healing ministry to the Samaritans (Acts 8:4–8).

SAUL /PAUL

- in his conversion (Acts 9:1–31).
- in his call to ministry (Acts 13:1–3).

- in his vision of ministry to Macedonia (Acts 16:6–10).
- in his freedom from jail (Acts 16:22–36).
- in his prediction of the outcome of the wreck of the ship on which he was being taken to Rome (Acts 27:13–44).

But the most remarkable example of Holy Spirit empowering in the New Testament does not involve the disciples but *Mary*, the mother of Jesus.

> [The angel said to her,] "You will be with child and give birth to a son, and you are to give him the name Jesus." . . . "How will this be," Mary asked the angel, "since I am a virgin?" The angel answered, "The Holy Spirit will come upon you, and the power of the Most High will overshadow you. So the holy one to be born will be called the Son of God" (Luke 1:31, 34–35).

If God calls you to do something, don't worry—He'll enable you to do it to His satisfaction.

One Final Promise

Let me leave you with a final promise from Hebrews 13:5, which is a quote from Deuteronomy 31:6—God the Holy Spirit will *never* leave you nor forsake you! The reason is that God loves you with a never-ending love (Jeremiah 31:3). You *can* leave Him or ignore Him, but He'll *always* be there waiting for *you* to come back to Him, the God of the Bible. You are *the only thing* that can separate you from God (Romans 8:38–39)!

4 GOD THE SON/MESSIAH

Contents

Develop Perspective on God the Son

Before reading this chapter, first bring your *own* perspective to the topic of "God the Son" by answering the following questions:

1. When did God the Son come into existence? When did He first appear on Planet Earth?
2. What does the Old Testament say about the coming of the Messiah? How did Jesus relate to those things said in the Old Testament about the coming of the Messiah?
3. Why is the genealogy of Jesus different in the book of Matthew than it is in the book of Luke?
4. Who was Melchizedek? What do you know about him?
5. What do you understand are the requirements for salvation? What do people have to do to be saved? What do you have to do to be saved?
6. Do you have to do anything to maintain your salvation? If yes, what? Can you lose your salvation? If yes, how? If no, why not?
7. Are there any unforgivable sins? If yes, what are they?
8. Has anything that you've been told about God the Son in church confused you or turned you off? Explain. (e.g., God arbitrarily picks and chooses who will and who won't be saved.)

Overview of the Chapter

- The *eternal existence* of God the Son is emphasized in this chapter and His manifestations in both the Old and New Testaments are described.
- The manner in which the life of Jesus *fulfilled* the Old Testament *prophecies* about Him is demonstrated.

- His *genealogy* is traced back to Adam, and the apparent inconsistency between the Matthew and Luke accounts is explained.
- Mankind's *need* for a Saviour is made clear.
- The *process* of salvation is spelled out in detail, including whether salvation is possible for those who have never heard the gospel message. The role of *repentance* in salvation is explained. Also, an explanation is given as to why the "Sin against the Holy Spirit" will not be forgiven.

Introduction: Manifestations of God the Son

It's important to remember that God the Son, like God the Father and God the Holy Spirit, has *always* existed; He is not of this world (John 8:23, 17:24). If you remember this, then it does not seem strange to say that the way God the Son *first* manifested Himself in *human* form was in the Old Testament as Melchizedek, King of Salem (Jeru*salem*) and High Priest of God, during the Old Covenant. Melchizedek was acknowledged as worthy of honour by Abraham, the first Hebrew, who was also an ancestor of the Jesus born in Bethlehem whose mother was Mary, the virgin wife of Joseph. Melchizedek is described as being *without beginning or end*, which can only be true of God (see Genesis 14:18–20 as explained in Hebrews 7:1–28). Hebrews 7:3 tells us that Melchizedek is "Without father or mother, without genealogy, without beginning of days or end of life, like the Son of God [Jesus] he remains a priest forever," and Psalm 110:4 prophesied the Messiah would be a priest forever in the order of Melchizedek. This notion of God the Son first appearing on earth as Melchizedek is not a new one—others have suggested the same thing.

However, His role as Saviour/Messiah/Christ in the New Testament (e.g., Acts 5:42) is the one of most interest to us here. Before looking at this role, let's accept that God the Son did not begin His *existence* here on earth—either as Melchizedek of

Salem or as Jesus of Nazareth. As Jesus told the Pharisees, "Before Abraham was born, I am" (John 8:48–59, cf. 5:17–18), a statement they understood as a claim for eternal Godhood co-equal with God the Father since Abraham had been born around 2000 years before Jesus and "I AM" is God's name (Exodus 3:14). The interlinear Bible in John 1:1 makes the godhood of the Son most explicit: "In [the] beginning was the Word [God the Son/Jesus], and the Word was with God, and *God was the Word*" (emphasis added).

Jesus' Life Foretold and Prophecy Fulfilled

The life of Jesus is foretold in the Old Testament, most fully portrayed as the suffering servant described in Isaiah 52:13–53:12. But there are many other specific prophecies that were made about Jesus the Messiah/Christ many years before His birth in a Bethlehem stable, all of which He fulfilled. Let's look at some of them.

PROPHECY	FULFILLMENT
1. **John the Baptist**	
Isaiah 40:3 – Someone in the wilderness calling "Prepare the way for the Lord."	Matthew 3:1–12 – John the Baptist went before the Lord in the spirit and power of Elijah.
Luke 1:11–17 – John the Baptist will go before the Lord in the spirit and power of Elijah	
Malachi 3:1, 4:5–6 – "Elijah" will be the messenger who will prepare the way for the Lord. This prophecy is still invoked in the Passover Seder.	Matthew 11:7–14 – John the Baptist is the "Elijah" who came and prepared the way for the Lord Jesus.
2. **Jesus' Parentage**	
Isaiah 7:14 – His mother would be a virgin.	Matthew 1:16–25 – Mary was a virgin, Jesus' real Father was God, Joseph was a descendant of King David, Jesus or Joshua means "The Lord Saves [us by
Isaiah 9:6–7 – He would be God's Son.	

PROPHECY	FULFILLMENT
Jeremiah 23:5–6, 30:9, 33:15–16 – He would be called "The Lord Our Righteousness" and would be descended from King David.	His Righteousness]."
3. **Jesus' Birthplace**	
Micah 5:2, Matthew 2:1–6 – He would be born in Bethlehem.	Luke 2:1–7 – Jesus was born in Bethlehem.
4. **Jesus' Home**	
Isaiah 9:1–2 – He would be a great light in Galilee.	John 1:1–5, 14 – Jesus, the Word of God: the Light of the World.
Jeremiah 31:15 – The mothers of Israel would have a great sadness.	Matthew 2:13–23 – Herod had the newborns in Bethlehem killed *after* Jesus' departure for Egypt;
Hosea 11:1 – God would call His Son out of Egypt.	His home after Egypt was Nazareth, which is in Galilee.
5. **Jesus' Ministry**	
Zechariah 9:9 – He would bring salvation and ride like a king on a donkey into Jerusalem.	Matthew 28:18–20, John 12:12–16 – Jesus rode into Jerusalem on a donkey, like a king.
Deuteronomy 18:15–19 – God promises the Israelites a prophet to whom they must listen.	John 6:14 – the people recognize Jesus as the prophet promised in Deuteronomy.
Psalm 69:9 – He would be zealous for the House of God/temple.	John 2:13–17 – Jesus cleared the temple of merchants and non-worshipers.
Psalm 110:4 – He would be a priest forever in the order of Melchizedek.	Hebrews 7:11–28 – Jesus' eternal priesthood in the order of Melchizedek is recognized.
Psalm 118:22–23 – Jesus will be the cornerstone.	Matthew 21:42–46, Acts 4:8–12 – both Jesus and His disciples proclaim Him the cornerstone.
Isaiah 42:6, Joel 2:28–32 – He would bring a new covenant that would include everyone—the Gentiles/non-Jews as well as the Jews—and involve the Holy Spirit.	Acts 10:34–46, Hebrews 8:6, 9:15 – Jesus brought the New Covenant and the Holy Spirit fell on those Gentiles listening to Peter tell them about it.
Isaiah 61:1–3 – the Spirit of God was to be upon Him and He was to preach the Good News to the poor and free the captives of sin.	Matthew 3:16–17, Luke 4:16–21 – the Spirit of God came upon Him and Jesus proclaimed His ministry of freedom for sin's captives.

PROPHECY	FULFILLMENT
Zechariah 11:10–13 – He would be betrayed for thirty pieces of silver.	Matthew 26:14–16, 47–50, 27:3–10 – He was betrayed for thirty pieces of silver.
6. **Jesus' Death and Resurrection**	
Exodus 12:46 - the bones of the Passover sacrifice were not to be broken.	John 19:28–37 – They did not break any of His bones but pierced His side after He died.
Zechariah 12:10 – He would be pierced.	
Psalm 22:18 – they would cast lots for His clothes.	Luke 23:32–34 – They cast lots for His clothes.
Isaiah 52:13–53:12 – The suffering servant would be pierced, wounded and die for the sins of humankind, be called a transgressor and buried in a rich man's tomb.	Luke 22:37 – He was called a transgressor.
	Luke 22:63–65 – He was beaten and mocked.
	Matthew 27:57–60 – He was buried in a rich man's tomb.
Psalm 16:10 – God the Father won't let His Holy One see decay.	Matthew 28:1–7 – Jesus was resurrected: raised from the dead.
	Acts 1:9–11 – Jesus was taken up into Heaven.
Isaiah 25:8–9 – He will swallow up death and remove the disgrace of sin.	Romans 6:23 – Jesus freed us from the penalty for our sins (hell).
	1 Corinthians 15:12–28, 50–57 – We will also be raised from the dead.
Zechariah 9:11 – He will free the prisoners from hell.	Matthew 27:50–54 – after Jesus died, many holy people who had died were raised to life.

The Genealogy of Jesus

The books of Matthew and Luke each give the genealogy of Jesus but appear inconsistent. One common way of resolving this inconsistency has been to say Matthew's version traces Christ's ancestry from Joseph, His earthly "father," and Luke's traces it through Mary, His earthly mother. However, since both make reference to Joseph and neither refers to Mary's ancestry, this will not do.

Before we look at this apparent inconsistency, let's carefully compare the two accounts. Matthew's account begins with Abraham and goes in chronological order to Joseph, whereas Luke's account begins with Joseph and goes in reverse chronological order back to Adam. I have redone Luke's account in chronological order to simplify the comparison.

MATTHEW 1:1-17	LUKE 3:23-38
	1. Adam, the son of God
	2. Seth, the son of Adam
	3. Enosh, the son of Seth
	4. Kenan, the son of Enosh
	5. Mahalalel, the son of Kenan
	6. Jared, the son of Mahalalel
	7. Enoch, the son of Jared
	8. Methuselah, the son of Enoch
	9. Lamech, the son of Methuselah
	10. Noah, the son of Lamech
	11. Shem, the son of Noah
	12. Arphaxad, the son of Shem
	13. Cainan, the son of Arphaxad
	14. Shelah, the son of Cainan
	15. Eber, the son of Shelah
	16. Peleg, the son of Eber
	17. Reu, the son of Peleg
	18. Serug, the son of Reu
	19. Nahor, the son of Serug
	20. Terah, the son of Nahor
21. Abraham	21. Abraham, the son of Terah
22. Isaac, the son of Abraham	22. Isaac, the son of Abraham
23. Jacob, the son of Isaac	23. Jacob, the son of Isaac

MATTHEW 1:1-17	LUKE 3:23-38
24. Judah, the son of Jacob	24. Judah, the son of Jacob
25. Perez, the son of Judah	25. Perez, the son of Judah
26. Herzon, the son of Perez	26.
27. Ram, the son of Herzon	27. Ram, the son of Perez
28. Amminadab, the son of Ram	28. Amminadab, the son of Ram
29. Nashon, the son of Amminadab	29. Nashon, the son of Amminadab
30. Salmon, the son of Nashon	30. Salmon, the son of Nashon
31. Boaz, the son of Salmon	31. Boaz, the son of Salmon
32. Obed, the son of Boaz	32. Obed, the son of Boaz
33. Jesse, the son of Obed	33. Jesse, the son of Obed
34. David, the son of Jesse	34. David, the son of Jesse
35. Solomon, the son of David He was the head of his family, of whom Nathan was a brother (2 Samuel 5:14; 1 Chronicles 3:5, 14:4). The line identified by Matthew from Solomon on is the royal line—the heads of the family of David down to Joseph, the "father" of Jesus. See also 1 Chronicles 3:10–24.	35. Nathan, the son of David He was also, like Solomon, a son of David by Bathsheba (2 Samuel 5:14; 1 Chronicles 3:5, 14:4); Zechariah 12:10–14: the clans of David, Nathan, Levi (the priesthood) and Shimei (the Gershonite clan of Levi responsible for the tabernacle during the Exodus, as described in Numbers 3:21–26) mourn for the pierced one, a clear messianic reference. The only reason to include Nathan and exclude Solomon is Nathan's messianic connection.
36. Rehoboam, the son of Solomon	36. Mattatha, the son of Nathan
37. Abijah, the son of Rehoboam	37. Menna, the son of Mattatha
38. Asa, the son of Abijah	38. Melea, the son of Menna
39. Jehosophat, the son of Asa	39. Eliakim, the son of Melea
40. Jehoram, the son of Jehosophat	40. Jonam, the son of Eliakim
41. Uzziah, the son of Jehoram	41. Joseph, the son of Jonam
42. Jotham, the son of Uzziah	42. Judah, the son of Joseph
43. Ahaz, the son of Jotham	43. Simeon, the son of Judah
44. Hezekiah, the son of Ahaz	44. Levi, the son of Simeon
45. Manasseh, the son of Hezekiah	45. Matthat, the son of Levi
46. Amon, the son of Manasseh	46. Jorim, the son of Matthat
47. Josiah, the son of Amon	47. Eliezer, the son of Jorim
48. Jeconiah, the son of Josiah	48. Joshua, the son of Eliezer

<table>
<tr><th>MATTHEW 1:1-17</th><th>LUKE 3:23-38</th></tr>
<tr><td>49. Shealtiel, the son of Jeconiah</td><td>49. Er, the son of Joshua</td></tr>
<tr><td>50. Zerubbabel, the son of Shealtiel</td><td>50. Elmadam, the son of Er</td></tr>
<tr><td>51. Abiud, the son of Zerubbabel</td><td>51. Cosam, the son of Elmadam</td></tr>
<tr><td>52. Eliakim, the son of Abiud</td><td>52. Addi, the son of Cosam</td></tr>
<tr><td>53. Azor, the son of Eliakim</td><td>53. Melki, the son of Addi</td></tr>
<tr><td>54. Zadok, the son of Azor</td><td>54. Neri, the son of Melki</td></tr>
<tr><td>55. Akim, the son of Zadok</td><td>55. Shealtiel, the son of Neri</td></tr>
<tr><td>56. Eliud, the son of Akim</td><td>56. Zerubbabel, the son of Shealtiel</td></tr>
<tr><td>57. Eleazer, the son of Eliud</td><td>57. Rhesa, the son of Zerubbabel</td></tr>
<tr><td>58. Matthan, the son of Eleazer</td><td>58. Joanan, the son of Rhesa</td></tr>
<tr><td>59. Jacob, the son of Matthan</td><td>59. Joda, the son of Joanan</td></tr>
<tr><td>60. Joseph, the son of Jacob</td><td>60. Josech, the son of Joda</td></tr>
<tr><td>61. Jesus, the “son” of Joseph</td><td>61. Semein, the son of Josech</td></tr>
<tr><td rowspan="13">Note: Luke would not make a mistake in naming the father of Joseph, since that would have been common knowledge in his day. The only reasonable explanation of the difference in the two genealogies is the one given above under Solomon/Nathan, i.e., that Matthew traces the royal line after King David and Luke traces the direct line of actual descent from King David. This is not an original idea—others have suggested the same thing (See NIV Study Bible, 1543, commentary on Luke 3:23-38).</td><td>62. Mattathias, the son of Semein</td></tr>
<tr><td>63. Maath, the son of Mattathias</td></tr>
<tr><td>64. Naggai, the son of Maath</td></tr>
<tr><td>65. Esli, the son of Naggai</td></tr>
<tr><td>66. Nahum, the son of Esli</td></tr>
<tr><td>67. Amos, the son of Nahum</td></tr>
<tr><td>68. Mattathias, the son of Amos</td></tr>
<tr><td>69. Joseph, the son of Mattathias</td></tr>
<tr><td>70. Jannai, the son of Joseph</td></tr>
<tr><td>71. Melki, the son of Jannai</td></tr>
<tr><td>72. Levi, the son of Melki</td></tr>
<tr><td>73. Matthat, the son of Levi</td></tr>
<tr><td>74. Heli, the son of Matthat
These direct descendents are of humble stock—their only mention in the Bible is here in Luke.</td></tr>
<tr><td>60. Joseph, the son of Jacob</td><td>75. Joseph, the son of Heli</td></tr>
<tr><td>61. Jesus, the “son” of Joseph</td><td>76. Jesus, the “son” of Joseph</td></tr>
</table>

The line through Matthew represents the “royal line”—the kingly or head of family line—and so, not surprisingly, most of the names from Rehoboam on are mentioned in a number of other places in the Bible. On the other hand, the Luke account records the actual lineage of Jesus. Since the only place in the Bible that the line from Mattatha to Heli is mentioned is here in Luke, an obvious question would be Where did Luke get his information? In those days, the genealogies of all the families were kept in the Temple in Jerusalem, so they could be checked. Being a genuine Israelite in Old Testament times was a "big deal," as reading 1 Chronicles 9:1–34; Ezra 8:1–14, 10:18–44; and Nehemiah 7:6–66, 10:1–28, 11:1–12:36 reveals. In 70 AD, the Temple and its contents were destroyed by order of the Roman Emperor Trajan, which included all of those genealogical records. One consequence of the destruction of those records is that, after 70 AD, it would be impossible for any new claimants to messiahship or priesthood to verify or validate their genealogies and so make their claims completely "kosher."

The Need for a Saviour / Redeemer

Mankind's need for redemption made clear

The covenant God made with Abraham required perfection—perfect adherence to all of God's commands—in order to attain salvation and entrance to heaven. For the approximately 2,000 years from the time of the establishment of that covenant until the death of Jesus, the Jews tried to fully abide by the terms of that covenant without success. Not one Jew was able to do it. No one met the terms of God's covenant with Abraham, codified by Moses into 613 commandments 430 years later (Galatians 3:17). Is this why a suffering Job longed to see Emmanuel and spend eternity with Him (Job 19:25–27)? As Proverbs 20:9 and Romans 3:10 remind us, there are no perfect people. And failure of perfect adherence requires atonement. Leviticus, especially chapter 16, explains it well:

> "But the goat chosen by lot as the scapegoat shall be presented alive before the Lord to be used for making atonement by sending it into the desert as a scapegoat. . . . [Aaron the priest] is

> to lay both hands on the head of the live goat and confess over it all the wickedness and rebellion of the Israelites—all their sins—and put them on the goat's head. He shall send the goat away into the desert. . . . The goat will carry on itself all their sins to a solitary place . . . in the desert" (10, 21–22).

The scapegoat is an archetype for Jesus, who atoned for the sins of the world (see also Numbers 29:11; Deuteronomy 21:22–23; Proverbs 16:6; John 18:32, 19:18; Romans 3:24–25, 6:10; 2 Corinthians 5:21; Galatians 3:22; Colossians 1:13, 2:13–14, Hebrews 10:10). Today, the "scapegoat" favoured by the more orthodox Jews is the chicken, an explicit recognition of their ongoing need for atonement.

However, as Hebrews 10:1–4 tells us, animal sacrifice does not really atone for the sins of people. In Old Testament times, it was well accepted by most middle-eastern religions that sin—offending the gods—required atonement, or payment of the penalty for sin. When you sinned, it was understood that you died spiritually. However, people also understood that you could get back into the good graces of the offended gods through a sacrifice: letting the physical life of the sacrificed creature atone for, or buy back, your spiritually dead life.

The requirement of atonement for sin has not changed, but our acceptance of the concept has, even though sin is just as common today as it's always been. But sin is no less *bad* than it has ever been: the person that sins is spiritually dead (Ezekiel 18:20), condemned to eternity in hell unless their sin is atoned for.

So how could imperfect people ever really atone for their sins? Only by a perfect human being giving His life for theirs. This is what God the Son did as Jesus Christ the Messiah. Let me make this very clear: God the Son, as Jesus Christ the Messiah, *came to die for all of humankind.* That was the purpose of Emanuel's visit to Earth! He was not "taken out" by the Jews or Romans, He was not defeated by Satan, and He was not an unwilling or an unwitting victim—He deliberately gave His life because He was *the only one* who could atone for the sins of humankind (Galatians 1:3–4).

Jesus spoke of His death many times. In Matthew there is the sign of Jonah, an allusion to His death (12:40); a prediction of His death and rebuke of Peter who didn't want to hear such a prediction (16:21–23); and more predictions of His death (20:17–19, 26:1–2). In the book of John, He said He would be "lifted up," an allusion to His death (3:14–15, 8:28–29, 12:32); His flesh would be given for the life of the world (6:51); He is the good shepherd who lays down His life for His sheep (10:11, 15); this was His time to be glorified, and His statement that unless a kernel of wheat dies, it remains fruitless, both allusions to His death (12:23–24).

The most unambiguous statement about Jesus' death being His mission is in John 10:17–18: "The reason my Father loves me is that *I lay down my life*—only to take it up again. *No one takes it from me, but I lay it down of my own accord.* I have authority to lay it down and authority to take it up again. This command I received from my Father" (emphasis added).

In John 19:30 Jesus tells us His mission is finished! On that basis, His victory should be celebrated both on Good Friday, as the perfect man sacrifice, and on Easter Sunday, for His resurrection, which is the assertion both of His Godhood and of His victory over sin and death (Hebrews 12:2). As Jesus said on the *first* Good Friday, "It is *finished*" (John 19:30, emphasis added). For Him *not* to die would have been defeat. Think of the crucifixion as the end of a cosmic hostage drama: we humans were the hostages because of sin, and the life of the Messiah was the freely given ransom payment for our redemption—not an accident or unfortunate incident, but a deliberate and necessary act planned by God the Father to open up the gates of heaven for us all. The engineer is not responsible for the death of a person who jumps on the train tracks in front of the speeding locomotive. Jesus got Himself crucified to be mankind's scapegoat.

Jesus' sacrifice and its significance

Let me chronicle the events of that sacrifice. It begins when "Jesus said 'It is finished.' With that He bowed His head and gave up His spirit" (John 19:30). Right after we see:

> At that moment the curtain of the temple was torn in two from top to bottom [*the end of the Old/Abrahamic Covenant*]. The earth shook and the rocks split. The tombs broke open and the bodies of many holy people who had died were raised to life. They came out of the tombs, and after Jesus' resurrection they went into the holy city and appeared to many people (Matthew 27:51–53).

This was the *start of the new covenant* that had been promised in Jeremiah 31:31–34 (see also Hebrews 8:7–13, 9:28, 10:14–18.). Jesus *opened up heaven for all humankind* in the past, present, or future who follow God's "still small voice"! Prior to Jesus' sacrifice, *no one was in heaven*, as John 3:13 tells us. Now let's now go over the salvation process.

The Process of Salvation

Second Peter 3:9 tells us that God wants no one to perish. Ezekiel 18:20 tells us that the soul who sins shall die. Since everyone dies physically, we know this means spiritual death. Revelation 20:12–15 tells us that at the end of all life on earth—the final judgment—the names of all those people who are saved will be found written in the Book of Life. This gives us a context within which to understand the process of salvation.

1. All people are born saved

Life begins at conception. If the fertilized ovum miscarries, the unborn foetus is aborted, or the young child dies before he or she is able to make a sinful choice—before the age of reason (Deuteronomy 1:39)—since they have not sinned, they are saved from hell and eternal damnation unto eternal life in heaven. Therefore, their name must have been written into the Book of Life at *conception*.

2. All people sin who reach the age of reason or accountability

First Kings 8:46 and Romans 3:23 instruct us that every (accountable) person has sinned. Therefore, once the age of reason is reached, all people *lose their initial salvation.*

3. God has provided the means for all sinners to be saved

John 3:16–17 tells us that God so loved humankind that he sent His only begotten Son, Jesus, to atone for all the sins of humankind for all time. This Jesus did by giving up his life on the cross as described in John 19:30.

4. Is there an unforgivable sin?

In Matthew 12:22–32, Mark 3:20–30 and Luke 12:10, Jesus speaks of the unforgiveable sin, the *Sin against the Holy Spirit.* To help you understand why this sin is unforgivable, let me quote directly from Matthew 12:22–24:

> Then they brought him a demon-possessed man who was blind and mute, and Jesus healed him, so that he could both talk and see. All the people were astonished and said, "Could this be the Son of David [Messiah]?" But when the Pharisees heard this, they said, "It is only by Beelzebub [Satan], the prince of demons, that this fellow drives out demons."

In verses 25–29 Jesus shows the absurdity of accusing Satan, the prince of demons, of driving out his fellow demons or fighting against himself. Finally, in verses 31–32 Jesus says,

> And so I tell you, every sin and blasphemy will be forgiven men [people], but the blasphemy against the Spirit will not be forgiven. Anyone who speaks a word against the Son of Man [Jesus, God the Son] will be forgiven, but anyone who speaks against the Holy Spirit will not be forgiven, either in this age or in the age to come [at the end of the world].

Mark 3:30 explains that Jesus said this because the Pharisees said He had an evil spirit (rather than the Holy Spirit).

The *Sin against the Holy Spirit*, as illustrated in these verses from Matthew and Mark (see also Luke 11:14–20), is to see the work of God but to ascribe it to another—to the Devil or to someone else (for instance, yourself). The reason that this sin is unforgivable is that God is showing *you* that He is real and that you need to repent and start following Him *now*! And it's not that God *won't* forgive you—it's that your "hardness of heart" or pride will keep you from acknowledging your need to repent and *ask* for forgiveness. Jesus was showing the Pharisees that He was God by the miracles He performed to deliberately draw them to God, and they stubbornly chose to ignore it . . . to their eternal peril!

God delivered me from alcoholism at the age of 40. If I had claimed my deliverance from alcoholism at age 40 was due to "willpower" rather than a miraculous gift from God, that would have been a sin against the Holy Spirit, for that deliverance was from God showing me that He was real and that I needed to change my life's direction. Again, the reason that this sin is unique is that it represents *you* ignoring God when He is speaking to you to bring along the road to *your* salvation!

5. Why did Jesus have to die?

A perfect human had to offer his life to truly atone for the sins of humankind and redeem us from spiritual death. That perfect human was Jesus.

6. What about those who have never heard of Jesus (both before and after his death)?

The ones who died before Jesus but who would have been saved if they'd had the chance because they'd listened to God's "still small voice" were saved. Luke 16:22–26 briefly describes the Limbo where they were, and Matthew 27:51–53 describes their release after the crucifixion. But what about the Muslims, Jews, Buddhists, Hindus, Animists, Paganists, etc. since then who have never heard the good news about salvation? These are God's prodigal sons and daughters—His from birth (Luke 15:11–32). John 14:6 tells us that Christ is The Way and 10:16 speaks of His "other sheep not of this pen." But if God is not willing that any should perish and these other people have never heard the good news of salvation, then how can they be saved, since they've never heard the gospel message preached and, having reached the age of reason, they have sinned and so lost their initial salvation?

J. I. Packer writes on the possibility of their salvation in his referenced article. This apparent dilemma is only a problem for humans, not God. Missionaries have told me about Jesus appearing to people they visited long before they, the missionaries, arrived. God does not *need* humans to save other human beings. But many evangelicals believe that Christian missionary work is *essential* to the salvation of the lost, since it is seen as a pre-condition to Christ's Second Coming (Mark 13:10). This is an example of the sin of *pride*. God has many means to work His many plans (e.g., Esther 4:12–16), including His plans for salvation. Sometimes God allows people to play an important role, but they are *never* essential! In fact, human beings *never* save other human beings—only God does.

The Holy Spirit has always been active and so is still active today; God is the same God He has always been and always will be, as Hebrews 13:8 tells us. Isaiah 30:21 says that God speaks The Way to all people; all they have to do is *listen*—to not listen is the Sin against the Holy Spirit! In other words, *people do not have to have an Acts 4:12 or Romans 10:9 "confessing Jesus as Lord" experience in order to be saved*! Of course, that's one way—but it's not always necessary, as illustrated by the following.

God's Call

Let me give another personal example to illustrate God speaking The Way to a person in a manner that was *not* an Acts 4:12/Romans 10:9 experience. I was a student at McGill University in 1959. At the time, I believed that people were only biological machines; I also believed that I was in love with a Roman

Catholic girl whom I was dating. God's "still small voice" spoke to me one day as I was walking along Sherbrooke St. in front of McGill. He told me, "Machines can't love." I now believe that God put the thought in my head, but at the time, I was sure I'd heard a voice, looked around, and saw that no one was anywhere near me. God had shown me The Way, and I took it. I was taking instruction in the Roman Catholic faith at the time because that was the price for dating a sincere believer, and after that encounter with God, I became genuinely interested and converted from nominal Protestantism to Roman Catholicism at the age of 21. However, repeated confessions of the same sins convinced me that I'd never make it to heaven since I'd never be good enough, so after ten years, I gave up trying. I was ready for salvation by grace (Ephesians 2:8–9), but it took me yet another ten years to actually get saved.

I believe that if you are obeying God's still small voice and walking the narrow road (Matthew 7:13-14), you *will* be saved, even if you haven't yet made that formal commitment. So, for example, if I had died during the time when I was being saved, I would have been heaven-bound. First Corinthians 1:18 speaks of "us who are being saved." I believe that I was *being saved* from the time God spoke to me when I was 20 and *I embarked on the narrow way* to when I actually accepted Christ as my saviour at age 40. I say that I was "being saved" because I *continued to seek* The Way during that time and again listened to the Holy Spirit's call at age 40 when I made my actual decision to accept Jesus Christ as my personal saviour (Lamentations 3:25–27). If I had rejected God's call, of course, that would have been a sin against the Holy Spirit, as explained previously.

Another call of God that I was privileged to hear about when new to the faith was the testimony given by a woman in Danny Paul's Sunday school class that I was then attending. As an adolescent in India, she heard about God from Christian classmates in school and became curious. However, to turn her back on her Hindu culture would mean social ostracism from family and friends, a very serious step. In making her decision, she prayed for a week to the goddess Kali, desperately asking her for a sign, but with *no* response. Finally, at the end of that fruitless week, she prayed to God and *immediately* got her sign. Psalm 53:2 tells us God *always* looks for those seeking Him. Now she knew which god was real, but she waited until her social circumstances were more favourable before she was ready to show her faith to the friends, family, and the world.

A third call, described by Moll in *Great Leap Forward* (33), was to Ruth, a devout Buddhist, who heard a voice in her mind telling her to believe in Jesus. Such calls are not unusual, but are rather the norm, as Jesus said in John 6:44–45. If you heed that call, you'll become more loving, as Romans 5:5 and 1 John 4:7 tell us. And after you've heeded that call, according to Psalm 32:1–2, you'll be blessed.

7. Just what does a salvation decision do for you?

Let me begin my explanation by comparing it with another decision—the marital decision. In the traditional marriage ceremony, the couple vow to love each other "for as long as they both shall live," but the divorce statistics show that, just as often as not, that vow is broken. It is no different with "asking Jesus into your heart." You may *hope* it's forever, but your lifestyle and whether or not you continue to listen to God's counsel show whether your "commitment to Christ" is still operational. Remember, it's not "once saved, always saved"; it's only for as long as you follow the leading of God's "still small voice" and continue to repent of your sins. If you stop, then you are ending the relationship. In speaking to the saved, John explains it best when he writes,

> If we claim to be without sin, we deceive ourselves and the truth is not in us. If we confess our sins, he is faithful and just and will forgive us our sins and purify us from all unrighteousness. If we claim we have not sinned, we make him [God] out to be a liar and his word has no place in our lives (1 John 1:8–10).

Jesus did not change the process of *ongoing salvation maintenance*; He opened the gates of heaven to allow people in. And that is what you acknowledge when you accept Jesus Christ as your personal Saviour—you acknowledge the once for all sacrificial atonement of the Messiah or Christ for *your own personal sins*, which sacrifice opens up the gates of heaven for *you personally*! But be clear: that acknowledgement, while it wipes your past sin slate clean, does not give you a once and for all "get into heaven free" pass. God *will* forgive all your future sins as well, but you *must first confess* the *serious* ones (Proverbs 28:13, Isaiah 30:15, 1 John 1:8–10) and repent of them, choosing to live differently. And there's no need for you to worry about which ones are serious—either you'll just know it or else the Holy Spirit will convict you by giving your conscience a nudge (1 John 3:19–21).

A word of comfort to the perfectionists reading this: *Don't beat yourself up for each and every one of your shortcomings*! When I say "serious sins," I mean "serious sins." The little imperfections all people display every day are *not* serious sins. Ordinary everyday failings are *not* important! So how can you tell if your sin is important enough to do something about? Very simply: if you manifest a *significant lack of love*, then that, and only that, is serious!

The next two sections describe both ways that you can lose your salvation after having embarked on the narrow way or made your salvation decision.

8. Can a person lose their salvation through neglecting to repent of sins committed (sins of commission)?

Just as the unsaved can *reject* God's call, the saved can *again turn their back* on God (1 John 5:16–17). Hebrews 6:4–6 and 10:26–31 show the consequences of people continuing to commit sins after being saved but remaining unrepentant (cf. 2 Peter 2:21). Exodus 32:32–33 and Deuteronomy 29:20 speak of, and 2 Chronicles 15:2 implies, names being blotted out of the Book of

Life for unrepented sin. Revelation 3:5 also describes the possibility of a person losing their salvation by their name being blotted out of the Book of Life.

Let's look at two examples:

1. In the Old Testament, we have the tragic saga of King Saul. Let me trace his story from the book of 1 Samuel. In 10:1 the prophet Samuel anoints him leader of Israel, in 10:9–11 the Holy Spirit comes upon him, and in 10:20–24 and 11:12–15 he's made king of Israel. In 11:1–11 the Spirit of God comes upon Saul and gives him a military victory. In 13:1–14 Saul commits the sin of disobedience against God because of impatience, which he rationalizes but from which he does not repent. Again, in 15:1–33 Saul rebels against God's command, this time for material gain, and God rejects him as king. This time, though, Saul is remorseful but obviously unrepentant (15:24–26), and Samuel tells him in 15:23, "For rebellion is like the sin of divination [foretelling the future using witchcraft], and arrogance like the evil of idolatry [making something more important than God]. Because you have rejected the word of the Lord, he has rejected you as king." In 16:1–13, David is designated as Saul's successor and in 16:14 these tragic words are recorded: "Now the Spirit of the Lord had departed from Saul, and an evil spirit from the Lord [i.e., God gave Satan access to Saul] tormented him." In 18:10–11 that evil spirit gets him to try and kill David, and Saul tries many more times to kill David as well (19:1– 26:25). In 28:1–25 Saul consults with a witch and is again rebuked by a "resurrected Samuel" for his disobedience and told that he will die "tomorrow," which he does (31:1–6). David knew better than to lose the Holy Spirit for unrepented sin (Psalm 51:11).

2. In the New Testament, Paul mentions the believer Demas as having deserted him because of his (Demas's) love of the world (2 Timothy 4:9, see also Colossians 4:14 and

> Philemon 23). Paul also mentions Hymenaeus, Alexander, Philetus and others who had wandered from the truth and were becoming more ungodly (1 Timothy 1:14–20, 5:15; 2 Timothy 2:16–19). This topic is anathema to Calvinists, who believe "once saved always saved."

Now let's look at how salvation can be lost not by a failure to repent of sin, but by a failure to love.

9. Can a person's salvation be taken away by sins of omission?

Arminians would have no trouble with the previous section but might struggle to accept this one. Your salvation can be lost not only by what you do, but also by what you *don't* do. Matthew 25:31–46, speaking of believers in terms of *sheep* and *goats*, says that some—the *goats* [unloving believers]—will *not* go to heaven.

> "I tell you the truth, whenever you did not do for [love] one of the least of these [people, which includes those who are hungry, thirsty, strangers, needing clothes, sick, or in prison], you did not do for me." Then they [the goats] will go away to eternal punishment, but the righteous [the *sheep*—loving believers] to eternal life (Matthew 25:45–46).

Let me make the meaning of this passage clear: it is *not* saying that you must love *all* the people who cross your path—only God can do that. It *is* saying, however, that you must love at least *some* of those people, and that includes *yourself*. The love that flows out of you testifies to your salvation and manifests itself in a love of God, yourself, and others. And it's not a *special effort* that you must make to love God, yourself, and others—it's something you *want* to do; something that *flows out of you* because of who you've become. A life that bears no fruit is one that the person treats just like a "salvation club" membership: once you're in you're safe and there's nothing else to do for the rest of your life. As the above shows, that's wrong-headed thinking. John refers to such believers in 1 John 3:18. If God speaks to you about this, heed His warning! (See also 2 Thessalonians 3:11–12 and James 2:12–13.)

10. Once you're saved, is it the end of fun in your life?

When I was contemplating becoming a "born again" Christian, one of the reasons I hesitated was because I believed that it was the end of whatever fun or enjoyment I would ever have in my life.[15] At that time I needed 66 oz. of liquor to get through each week, so I now wonder what enjoyment I was worried about losing! The belief that living the Christian life is "sackcloth and ashes"—the end of enjoyment in life—is one of the Devil's deceptions. If you follow God's leading, He will lead you into real happiness, and even joy, which is the result of abundant living.

Final Comments on Salvation

Some final comments about salvation and our Saviour, Jesus.

If you sincerely believe in reincarnation, universalism, or "once saved, always saved," please remember this: if I jump off the roof of a tall building because I sincerely believe that the law of gravity does not apply to me, I will be killed just as surely as if I *had* believed in it. The enduring truth of the process of salvation is unaltered by the sincerity of my lack of belief in it. Reality is unaffected by belief; there is no "placebo salvation." Also, "once saved, always saved" means you've lost your freedom of choice or, in other words, you've become a "saved robot." The ability to lose your salvation is not a negation of God's power; rather, it's an affirmation of the freedom of choice that God has given you and all humankind (Ezekiel 18:26, 33:18)!

---

[15] I discuss the abundant living that accompanies salvation in the next chapter in the section "Living the Life that's Best for You."

God the Son is the Gate to heaven for all humankind (John 10:9, 14:6).

In order to be saved, there are two options. The first is to become a Christian by accepting Jesus Christ as your personal saviour and receiving the Holy Spirit (John 7:39), an option only available in New Testament times since the Messiah's atonement and only utilized in fairly recent times, according to Hsu in *A Multifaceted Gospel*. The second option is to become a follower of The Way by following the leading of God the Holy Spirit's "still, small voice," an option available in both Old and New Testament times. (Note: this includes both those who make the salvation decision and those who are being saved but have not yet made the salvation decision.)

Whichever way you choose, God has not changed the process needed to maintain your salvation. In today's New Testament times, as in the Old Testament, you still need to continue to listen to God the Holy Spirit's "still small voice" speaking to your conscience about the need to repent of any serious sins and to love the God who already loves you as well as to love yourself and others. As Romans 8:14 says, if you're led by (i.e., *following*) the Spirit of God, you're a son (child) of God. In Matthew 7:13–14 and Luke 13:23–24, Jesus reminds us that few find the narrow way of eternal salvation because, as given in His explanation of the parable of the sower in Matthew 13:18–23, many things can throw us off track in this life. Why not "Seek the Lord while he may be found. . . . turn to . . . God, for he will freely pardon"(Isaiah 55:6–7)?

When saved, you are "born again," a term Jesus used in John 3:3–8. "Born again" can also be translated as "born from above" or "born of the [Holy] Spirit." This happens when you repent of your sins and accept Jesus' atoning sacrifice. That's what happened to His disciples in John 20:22.[16] The Holy Spirit indwells you or is "born" in you and you are reborn as a full-fledged adopted son or daughter of God—you are no longer one of God's prodigals.

---

[16] See chapter 3, "Characteristics of God the Holy Spirit," #6.

In the section on how Jesus fulfilled the Old Testament prophecies about the Messiah, I cited Isaiah 7:14, which says His mother would be a virgin. The word for "virgin" can also be translated as "young woman," and this has been used to argue that Mary was not necessarily a virgin. This argument is bogus on two grounds. First, in those days, young Israelite women *were* virgins, and second, Matthew 1:16–25 tells us that, in fact, Mary *was* a virgin.

Finally, Jesus is our *Judge* at the Final Judgement (John 5:21–30; Acts 17:29–31; Romans 2:5–8; 2 Corinthians 5:10; Revelation 20:11–15, 21:5–8, 22–27, 22:12–13). Therefore, believe and be saved—do not draw back and be destroyed (Hebrews 10:39)!

5 LIVING THE LIFE THAT'S BEST FOR YOU IS PLEASING TO GOD

Contents

Develop Perspective on Living the Best Life

Before reading this chapter, first bring your *own* perspective to the topic of "Living the Best Life" by answering the following questions:

1. Is the life that's pleasing to God one of sober serious living or one that's happy, joyous, and free? Explain.
2. What's the most important requirement for leading an abundant/full/fulfilled life?
3. Will you be wealthy if you are living abundantly? What are God's views about wealth?
4. As you become a disciple of God, what are some of the things that you can expect to happen to you?
5. What's more important: having faith in God and really knowing the Bible or being a loving person? Explain.
6. Which should you strive for first: *holiness*—obeying the commandments of God for leading a righteous life—or *love*? Why?
7. Has anything that you've been told in church about living the life that's best for you confused you or turned you off? Explain. (e.g., were you told there were a lot of rules to follow?)

Overview of the Chapter

- Love is of critical importance. Explanations are given on how to love one's enemies, the difference between self-love and selfishness, and the vital importance of loving oneself. The relationship between love and holiness is used to understand the failure of the pharisaical lifestyle.

- Living the life that's best for you is boiled down to love. The fruit of the spirit are related back to love. Abundant living is also explained.
- Spiritual growth and discipleship are explored. The views of C. S. Lewis and A. W. Tozer on discipleship are presented.

Introduction: Understanding Love

According to Rabbinical scholars, there are 613 commandments defined by God in the Old Testament. However, as noted in chapter 2, Jesus boiled all 613 down to only two, which are:

> Love God with all your heart, soul, mind and strength, and
> Love your neighbour as [you already love] yourself.

This is known as the Great Commandment and is contained in all three of the synoptic gospels (Matthew 22:35–39, Mark 12:28–34, Luke 10:25–28).

In other words, the key is:

Love

The hymn "Jesus *Loves* Me" is one of the few things that stuck with me from my early church and Sunday school days.

As we endeavour to love our neighbours as we love ourselves, it is important to remember that "others" doesn't mean just our families or people we like; it includes those we dislike and our *enemies*, as Jesus makes clear in Matthew 5:38–48 and Luke 6:27–38. I think an enemy common to most people in our society is the *violent offender*. How, in practical terms, can you be expected to love someone who rapes, physically assaults, or murders others? Does it mean being permissive with respect to such behaviour? And if not, what then?[17]

[17] Appendix 2 contains my "Position Paper on Dealing Effectively with Violent Offenders So As to Really Make Canada Safer," portions of which are referred to here.

Let's first understand the *profile* of the typical Canadian violent offender. He's a single white male with a dysfunctional family background who was first arrested as a juvenile and so has a record of prior incarceration. He's also a substance abuser who's unemployed, lacks a high school education, and has an unstable job history. He developed his violent tendencies through violence experienced in his home while growing up. The probability of his *recidivism* during his lifetime exceeds 80%, and mere incarceration slightly increases his likelihood of re-offending.

Obviously, to release a violent offender who still has violent tendencies and lacks the education and job skills to earn a decent living while still having a substance abuse problem is a recipe that ensures failure! The good news is that effective *rehabilitation* for the violent offender is available: his drug abuse can be treated, he can be provided with high school education and be taught an employable trade and, most importantly, his violent tendencies can be virtually eliminated. The violent offenders most difficult to rehabilitate are pedophiles and sexual predators. I believe that all two-or-more-time violent offenders should remain *incarcerated until judged rehabilitated* and that, I believe, is how you show *love* to these enemies. If they are never judged rehabilitated, they should never be released. It is unloving to the violent offender to release him if he's almost guaranteed to re-offend, to fail. It's also unloving to others—the community into which he's released—that will almost certainly experience his violence.

If you love yourself and others, you'll do what's best for yourself and others (James 2:8). Daniel 9:4 speaks of God's covenant of love with those who love Him. First Corinthians 8:3 says those who love God are known by God. First John 4 tells us:

> Everyone who loves has been born of God and knows God. Whoever does not love does not know God, because God is love (7b–8). . . . Whoever lives in love lives in God, and God in him (16b). . . . We love [God] because he first loved us (19). . . . If anyone says, "I love God," yet hates his brother [others], he is a liar. For anyone who does not love his brother [others], whom

> he has seen, cannot love God, whom he has not seen. And He has given us this command: Whoever loves God must also love his brother [others] (20–21).

Finally, 1 Corinthians 13:1–13 tells us that, without love, every other accomplishment or quality you have counts for *nothing*! If you are *not a loving Christian*, to call yourself a Christian at all is an *oxymoron*!

Self-love and Selfishness

In 2 Timothy 3:2 Paul speaks negatively of "lovers of themselves" or "self-lovers," and it's clear from the context he's speaking of *selfish* people and not self-lovers in the Matthew 22:39 sense. Many assume that self-love *is* selfishness, but nothing could be further from the truth. In 2 Timothy 3:2–7 Paul goes on to describe other characteristics of these *selfish* men: money-lovers, boastful, proud, abusive, disobedient to parents, ungrateful, unholy, *without love*, unforgiving, slanderous, without self-control, brutal, not loving good, treacherous, rash, conceited, pleasure-lovers not God-lovers, and taking advantage of women where they can.

As Paul indicates, a selfish person does what they feel like doing without regard for the consequences. Today, they get high on drugs or alcohol, drive a vehicle recklessly or at an unsafe speed, have sex with whomever they feel like—even without the other person's consent—steal, kill, and abuse themselves and others in many other ways. Selfish people don't respect themselves and the fact that their bodies can become Temples of the Holy Spirit (1 Corinthians 6:19). However, if you love yourself, you do what is best for yourself and avoid the bad: you don't drink to excess, you drive safely, and you don't have sex without the other person's consent or steal or kill, etc. You do that because that's how you'd want to be treated. The Golden Rule says, "So in everything, do to others what you would have them do to you, for this sums up the Law and the Prophets" (Matthew 7:12).

The Order of Loving

Evangelicals are told that the Christian order of love is: 1. God, 2. neighbour, and 3. self. This sounds noble—to love your neighbour before you love yourself seems unselfish—but it is a *lie from hell!* It is a form of *insanity*. It is the *archetype of co-dependency*. It is a *type of phariseeism*. If you do not love yourself, you *cannot* truly love others; you cannot give away what you do not have! Loving yourself *enables* you to love others. In the last 30 years of listening to sermons, I've only heard two, both on Love, which advocated loving yourself, one by Dennis Posno and the other by Charles Stanley. In Matthew 7:12 Jesus tells us to do to others as we would wish to have done to us, which is seen to sum up the message of Scripture to love God and to love your neighbour as you already love yourself.

In my experience, many, if not most, people, including Christians, do *not* love themselves. Do you love yourself? How can you tell if you love yourself? It's simple. If you *always do what is truly best for yourself*, then you *always love yourself*! Those times when you don't do what's best for you are when you are *not* loving yourself. So the best thing to do for yourself is to identify areas where you are *not* doing what's best for you and then do whatever it takes to overcome this "less than best" approach. And when you do this, you will also become more loving by doing what's best for others as well. This doesn't mean you'll be trying to control others; it means you won't think selfishly in areas that affect them but rather empathically—how would they be affected if I did that? In other words, as you become more aware of yourself and your own needs and feelings, you are sensitized to others and their needs and feelings.

Love and Holiness

The unique Christian message is that salvation is by grace—the unmerited favour of God—and not by works; no one ever has or ever will earn their salvation because they've lived a perfect life (Romans 3:23, 2 Corinthians 3:6, Ephesians 2:8–9). A holy person approaches perfection by attempting to live the divine ideal. This sounds pretty good; yet Jesus reserved His harshest criticism for the Pharisees, who were attempting to do just that. The reason is that they were hypocrites, looking good on the outside but pretty bad on the inside (Isaiah 29:13). But I'm sure most, if not all, of the Pharisees began sincerely in attempting to be good.

So how could they fail so miserably? One reason, noted by Yancey in a 2008 article, "The Benefits of Brokenness," is that confessing personal failures and admitting a daily need for grace is difficult for those who take pride in their independence and self-sufficiency. But the fundamental reason is this: if you attempt holiness *before* you know that God loves you and you love God, and before you also love yourself, you will *fail* miserably—you'll be just like the Pharisees. You'll be an unhappy, uptight, self-righteous, and judgmental person, working at making all around you as miserable and uptight as yourself.

As I see it, many Evangelical Christian leaders, who are today's orthodoxy just like the Pharisees were the orthodox leaders of their day, seem to fall into this category, a situation discussed by Yancey in *What's So Amazing About Grace*:

> . . . I asked if [this prostitute] had ever thought of going to a church for help. . . . "Church," she cried, "Why would I ever go there? I was already feeling terrible about myself. They'd just make me feel worse" (11). . . . The Pharisees had much in common with those whom the press might call Bible-belt fundamentalists today (196).

They begin with good intentions, but goodness that *precedes* love is doomed to failure! Graham, in *The Journey*, states:

> The Christian faith is [not] only a set of rules—a list of dos and don'ts to be obeyed. Sadly, some people see it that way, and their lives are joyless as a result. They are constantly trying to please God, forgetting that *the Christian faith isn't a set of rules but a relationship*—a personal, intimate, daily walk with the living God. When our faith becomes nothing more than a series of rules and regulations, joy flees (187).

If you read these sentences and find yourself gnashing your teeth, perhaps *you* also are a Pharisee (Acts 7:54)!

Yancey goes on to say:

> I think of the thousands of chapters based on the twelve-step program that meet . . . all across the nation, any night of the week. The Christians who founded Alcoholics Anonymous faced a choice: whether to make it a restrictively Christian organization or to found it on Christian principles and then set it free [for the Holy Spirit to control]. They chose the latter option, and now millions of people in America look to their program—based on dependence on a "Higher Power" [God of their understanding] and on a supportive [non-judgmental] community— as a remedy for addictions to alcohol, drugs, and food [and as a path to God] (267).

"HIGHER POWER"

The concept of "God as we understand Him" was hard to grasp. My family believed there is only one way to view God. My parents used religion to keep me in line. I believed we went to the only true church. There was a list of do's and don'ts. I was afraid of God, viewing Him as a severe judge just waiting to punish me.

By the end of my first meeting, I was impressed with the acceptance I felt. There was no gossip or criticism. People were friendly even though they had differing opinions and beliefs. No one tried to change others by telling them what to think or how to feel. In Al-Anon I felt for the first time as if I could be myself. I could relax and let a Higher Power of my understanding evolve.

I realized the God of my parents had come in a very small box, not expansive enough for me. I fired that God and hired a new one. My new Higher Power is much bigger than the old one. He loves me, cares for me, and accepts me just as I am—a work of art in progress. He is a God who wants the best for everyone. My Higher Power can turn tragedy into something positive, because out of my difficult childhood has come a God I no longer fear, but treasure. (*Hope for Today,* Virginia Beach: Al-Anon Family Groups Inc., 2002, p.297)

Many evangelicals object to the notion of "God as we understand Him," preferring instead to affirm belief in "the Christian God" or the characteristics of God affirmed by their particular denomination. However, this is bogus. In truth, *everyone* believes in a "God of their own understanding." Go to any church and ask the members to tell you about what God is like based on *their specific experiences* and, as I have, you'll hear many unique and heartfelt views about God rather than the standard doctrine provided by their denomination. Our personal experience, not stated doctrine, determines who and what God is for each of us—regardless of whether or not we go to church. *God for you is the God of your personal understanding, as He is for every human being on the face of the earth*! For heaven's sake, whose understanding do you carry around inside your head if not your own?

As a twice-divorced Christian, on Sunday, I attend a non-evangelical church, Collier United, pastored by Dennis Posno, where salvation is preached and a loving life is emphasized. I also attend two twelve step meetings each week, one inside a medium security penal institution.

One final quote from Philip Yancey on the topic:

> We in the church have as much to learn from people in the recovery movement as we have to offer them. I was struck by one observation from an alcoholic friend of mine. "When I'm late to church, people turn around and stare at me with frowns of disapproval. I get the clear message that I'm not as responsible as they are. When I'm late to AA, the meeting comes to a halt and everyone jumps up to hug and welcome me. They realize that my lateness may be a sign that I almost didn't make it. When I show up, it proves that my desperate need for them won over my desperate need for alcohol." ("Lessons from Rock Bottom", 72)

A final comment on love and holiness

John 14:15 quotes Jesus as saying, "If you love me, you will obey what I command [be holy]." The usual interpretation I've heard of this passage is that obedience proves the sincerity of your love: I obey therefore I love. I believe that interpretation is all *wrong*; in fact, it's got it *backwards*. The correct interpretation is that if you *do* love God plus yourself and others, you will *want* to live as God commands and try your *best* to do so because that's the way that's *best*—it results in the most joy for you and others! Love is the driver of your spirit: I love, *therefore I obey*. Alternatively, if you begin by obeying the commandments *before* you love, you are on your way to becoming a Pharisee!

Living the Life that's Best for You

How can anyone *dare* tell you what life is best for *you*! That's your decision alone! An automobile analogy helps us to understand this seemingly presumptuous claim. The car makers say it's best for a car to service it regularly—change the oil; check the brakes, engine, transmission, radiator, electrical system, etc.; and operate it properly—not exceed recommended speed, keep it clean, remove road salt, use recommended fuel, etc. So as a car owner, you *can* put water in the fuel tank instead of the recommended fuel, but it will damage your vehicle. Similarly, God, our designer, is able to specify the kind of life that's best for us humans. And it's not some joyless ritualized existence or going to church all the time or being "super-religious." That kind of life has been described as "being so 'heavenly-minded' that you're no earthly good." In fact, the kind of life that God wants for us is called the *abundant* (full or fulfilled) life.

Abundant Living

I described earlier that when I was contemplating becoming a "born again" Christian I hesitated because I was sure that whatever enjoyment I had had in my life was over and now it was "sackcloth and ashes" time. Since my enjoyment required the support of 66 oz. of liquor to get me through each week, whatever I was worried about losing could not have been very enjoyable! Today, I can honestly say I am much happier. I am actually *happy—content with my life—and I don't need to abuse substances* to be happy! God promises believers an abundant life (John 10:10), and increasingly, this *is* my experience.

Let me explain that "abundant living" is not Christian code for the "Prosperity Gospel." Yancey, in *Where Is God When It Hurts*, quotes an Eastern European Christian: "You Western Christians often seem to consider material prosperity to be the only sign of God's blessing" (98). I think the Prosperity Gospel is promoted by those made wealthy through ministry as a way of *rationalizing* their own prosperity (cf. 1 Peter 5:2, 2 Peter 2:3). If you work on what's *best* for God, yourself, and others, you'll have *real* abundant living.

God is not against wealth, it's just not a holiness enhancer (Proverbs 18:11). Jesus' messages on *not* gathering treasure here on earth (Matthew 6:19–24), against greed (Luke 12:15), the parable of the prodigal son (Luke 15:11–32), on the inability to serve both God and Money (Luke 16:13–15), and to the rich young man (Luke 18:18–30) make that clear. Jesus says, "What good will it be for a man if he gains the whole world, yet forfeits his soul?" (Matthew 16:26). Job, a wealthy man, tells us not to put our trust in money (Job 31:24–28). Solomon wasn't blessed by his wealth from God (1 Kings 3:1–15, Ecclesiastes 1:2). Proverbs 28:20 says don't be eager for wealth. Ecclesiastes 5:10 and 12 note those who love money never have enough and that wealth brings anxiety. First Timothy 6:9–10, 17 sees the desire for money as a trap; both Proverbs 11:28 and Revelation 3:17–18 warn against relying on wealth.

This is the *curse* of prosperity, as the Israelites found out: it leads to the idea "God's not necessary"—you can *buy* your own blessings, you *don't need God* to provide them (Jeremiah 17:9, Amos 6:1–7)! Yancey makes a similar observation in the September 2008 *My Daily Bread*. Perhaps this is why Jesus said "It is easier for a camel to go through the eye of a needle than for a rich man [person] to enter the kingdom of God [be saved and go to heaven]"

(Matthew 19:24). If you have lots of money, why do you need God at all? The answer is because God is the real root cause of your wealth—He makes it happen, *not* you! (Deuteronomy 8:18).

Abundant living leads to *real* prosperity and success (Proverbs 21:21). Galatians 5:6 says what really counts is faith expressed in love. Colossians 3:23–24 tells us to do our work with all our heart and receive God's reward. And Matthew 6:25–34 reminds us that we don't need to worry, for we are promised that if we seek God first, He'll take care of our needs. I've spoken to many people called to missionary work, *none* of whom became wealthy, yet through the hardships endured, *all* radiated with the glow of a close walk with God their provider.

To be successful and prosper in *your* walk with God, the "inner you" (your soul/spirit) must rule over the "outer you" (your physical and emotional desires). The greater your ongoing consciousness of God's presence and submission to His leading, the more your life will prosper and the more successful you'll be. You may or may not be wealthy, but you'll have love, joy, peace, etc.

Luke 17:20–21 explains that the Kingdom of God is *within you*—if you're following the leading of God the Holy Spirit as communicated by His "still small voice saying this is the way; walk in it." And this helps us understand the hereafter better. If you're following God's leading, you'll experience "heaven on earth," and if you're not, you'll experience "hell on earth." It's *your* choice! So if you've got a "helluva life" here on earth, ask God for some "heavenly help" and leave your misery behind—start living fruitfully! The only reason not to is because *you don't love yourself*!

Let me make it clear that people who do not love themselves are *not* that way because they lack intelligence or are inherently bad. They are that way because there is some pain from their dysfunctional past that they are trying to "numb out" and abuse of self and others is their way of numbing out. They will continue to "numb out" and lead painful selfish lives until they make their lives truly unmanageable, at which point they *may* become ready to admit their "powerlessness" over their lives in the area where their life is unmanageable, abandon their self-management, and look for God's help, as the twelve step programs describe in the first three steps.

Let me give a personal example.

In chapter 3, I discussed going to the "Communion with God" seminar and how it led me to love. What I didn't explain was what led me to that seminar in the first place. For the first ten years or so after my salvation experience, I was a conflicted individual: I was a shame-based perfectionist. A shame-based person is ashamed of who and what they are. This is not guilt. Guilt is remorse over what you've done but wish you hadn't, or not done but wish you had. Shame, on the other hand, is self-loathing, a belief that what and who you are is defective, inferior, or unworthy. That was me. My perfectionism was my attempt to compensate for what I believed to be my inherent inferiority. If I performed better than others and came closer to perfection, I could increase my self-worth and come closer to being "normal." None of this was done consciously or with awareness—if you had asked me if I was a shame-based perfectionist, I would have denied it, and I believe that most of the people who knew me then would also have denied it. As I saw it then, my imperfect wife and children added to my "God debt load"—if only they would do as I told them and become closer to the perfect ideal I saw for them, then at least my debt wouldn't get worse.

So one morning, I was lying in bed beside my wife, who was sleeping soundly, and I realized I was angry with her. Now, my being angry with her was not unusual; I was often angry with her and our two children. At that moment, however, because she was sleeping, the absurdity of being angry with her struck me. She had done nothing so far that day for me to get angry at! I believe at that moment the Holy Spirit inspired me to see that there were things going on inside of me that I didn't understand but that I needed to understand. So my road to healing began—first counselling, then "Communion with God" and twelve step groups: Adult Children of Alcoholics and Al-Anon. One of the wonderful things one of my counsellors, Joan Hyatt, a Christian, shared with me was: "Ken—I've got news for you. You're not worse than anyone else, and you're not better than anyone else. But you are just as good as everyone else."

One little aside: you may be wondering what would motivate anyone to disclose such painful details about themself. There are several reasons. First of all, these details are true. Secondly, they might help someone going through a similar experience. And thirdly, to keep them inside and be unwilling to share these details is to continue to be *ashamed* of myself and that part of my life! Self-disclosure is an important part of healing (The great apostle Paul calls himself the worst of sinners in 1 Timothy 1:15–16).

In Psalm 84:11 we're promised that "the Lord bestows favor and honor; no good thing does he withhold from those whose walk is blameless," and in Psalm 121:7–8 the promise is: "The Lord will keep you from harm—he will watch over your life; the Lord will watch over your coming and going both now and forevermore." God wants *you* to have an abundant life and will help you get it.

Sin and Fruitful Living

The 613 commandments in the Torah part of the Old Testament defined the dos and don'ts required of God's covenant people, the Hebrews. To disobey or unknowingly violate *any* of those commandments was to sin. All sin required atonement to restore the sinner's relationship with God. The Messiah simplified the commandment structure by boiling it down to loving God and loving others as you already love yourself. If you live like that, love, joy, peace, patience, kindness, goodness, faithfulness, gentleness, and self-control will flow out of you, as stated in Galatians 5:14, 22–23. In the film of Arthur Miller's *Death of a Salesman*, the salesman character implied in the title, Willy Loman (acted by Dustin Hoffman), seems to be happy with his life that includes affairs with "other women." But in a candid moment when he is with one of these "other women," he reveals his desperate loneliness. During the same episode with this woman, his son Biff catches him with her and sees his father for what they both know he is—a fake! And that's the way it is with *all* sinful living: it may be *exciting*, but it *won't really be satisfying* (Isaiah 48:22, 57:21).

Unfruitful living

In Luke 6:43, 45 Jesus states,

> No good tree bears bad fruit, nor does a bad tree bear good fruit. . . . The good man brings good things out of the good stored up in his heart, and the evil man brings evil things out of the evil stored up in his heart. For out of the overflow of his heart his mouth speaks.

James 1:13–15 explains:

> When tempted, no one should say, "God is tempting me." For God cannot be tempted by evil, nor does he tempt anyone; but each one is tempted when, by his own evil desire, he is dragged away and enticed. Then, after desire has conceived, it gives birth to sin; and sin, when it is full-grown, gives birth to death.

So, as Galatians 5:19–21 describes, if hatred, jealousy, fits of rage, *selfishness*, envy, etc. are what comes out of you, God's Spirit is not your resident counsellor.

Selfish is how people begin life—self-centred or ego-centric. You can watch a young child at play. They have difficulty sharing and get angry with things that do not behave as the child believes they ought. They are selfish. Most people as they develop and mature grow out of selfishness, but those who did not experience the love they needed as children or were abused as children often don't (e.g., dysfunctional adults and those suffering from Narcissistic Personality Disorder).

Let's now look in detail at the fruit of the spirit listed above. Since I have already mentioned love, I'll begin with joy and hope, which Paul adds to love and faith in 1 Corinthians 13:13.

Joy and Hope

Joy and happiness are not the same thing. People are happy when things go their way; when things don't, they are unhappy.

Joy, however, comes from within and is independent of circumstances. Nehemiah: 8:10 speaks of the joy of the Lord as our strength and Paul, in jail when he wrote his letter to the Philippians, in verses 4:11–13 called himself content *independent of his circumstances*. Then he tells us in Romans 14:17 that the source of our joy and his is the Holy Spirit.

In Romans 8:24–25 Paul speaks of hope as wishing for something we do not have. In 1 Peter 3:15b we're encouraged to "Always be prepared to give an answer . . . for the hope that you have. But do this with gentleness and respect." I believe that joyful people are hopeful and optimistic about the future because they trust in God. Gracie Allen, of Burns and Allen fame, is said to have spoken about the enduring quality of hope when you trust in God: "Never put a period where God has put a comma."

Peace and Patience

Isaiah 26:3 and John 16:33 tell us that the way to peace is to trust God. Colossians 3:15 counsels us to "Let the peace of Christ rule in your hearts, since as members of one body you were called to peace." Romans 12:18 and Hebrews 12:14 encourage us, if possible, to live at peace with everyone.

Isaiah 40:31, in the King James translation, reassures us about patience: "But they that wait upon the Lord shall renew their strength; they shall mount up with wings as eagles; they shall run, and not be weary; and they shall walk, and not faint." If I wait on God, I am trusting in His timing, and so I will have peace and patience.

Kindness and Goodness

In Ruth 2:5–23 Boaz, an ancestor of Jesus, showed kindness to Ruth because she had been good to her mother-in-law Naomi, who was a relative of his. Luke 10:30–35 tells the story of a Samaritan who was kind and good to a Jewish traveller. The Jewish traveller was a complete stranger to him and likely *disliked* Samaritans. Proverbs 14:31 says your kindness and good deeds honour God. Matthew 5:16 encourages you to "let your light [kindness and goodness] shine before men, that they may see your good deeds and praise your Father in heaven." In other words, your good and kind deeds draw people to *God.*

Faith and Faithfulness

Hebrew 11:1 defines faith for us: "Now faith is being sure of what we hope for and certain of what we do not see." Verses 3–40 give numerous examples of people who had great faith, many of whom did not receive what they had hoped for in their lifetime, yet they remained faithful—true to their belief or trust in God—so they had peace in their lives (Isaiah 26:3).

I believe our faith in a Loving God is most severely challenged when we personally experience suffering, when someone we love suffers or dies, or when we learn of a global tragedy that involves a great loss of life. We often think a loving God would surely intervene in those circumstances. But He does not, and we ask ourselves, "Why?"

When I have struggled with such thoughts, I have found it helpful to reflect on the fact that God chose not to intervene even in the case of His own Son, Jesus, who pleaded with God the Father to ease His suffering and to cancel His sacrificial death. But in spite of having His pleas denied, Jesus the man remained faithful to His heavenly Father to the end: His death on the cross, as related in Matthew 26:36–27:50.

Remember, since we saw in chapter 2 that the Trinity are *One*, and Jesus told us that He and the Father are *One* (John 10:30, 17:11; cf. Hosea 13:4), this means that, in some real sense, God the Father was a participant in Jesus' sacrificial offering of Himself. And, as His followers, Peter reminds us that Jesus is the example we also are to follow, even if our faithfulness is tested by suffering (1 Peter 2:21).

Gentleness and Self-Control

A gentle person is one who is meek and humble. Numbers 12:3 tells us that Moses was the most humble person on earth, and yet, this humble man seemed anything but meek in Exodus

32:7–32 as he dealt with the infidelity of the Israelites toward God. Similarly, Jesus told people He was gentle and humble of heart in Matthew 11:29, yet He appeared to be anything but meek in Matthew 21:12–13 as He drove out the commercial interests from the Temple, His Father's house, and in Matthew 23:1–36 when He denounced the hypocrisy of the Pharisees.

An understanding of the word "meek" gives us a clue to this apparent contradiction. *The Oxford Dictionary* defines it thus: "Free from *self-will*; piously humble and submissive; patient and unresentful" (emphasis added). Neither Moses nor Jesus acted from human self-will, but rather, were doing the will of God; "self-control" was really God-controlled motivation. Their egos were absent from their actions. Second Timothy 2:24–26 reinforces this notion of ego-absence in dealing with opposition.

Let me conclude this piece on the fruit of the spirit by citing Colossians 3:12–14, which tells us that *love* binds all the fruit of the spirit together in unity.

Discipleship

What does it mean to be a disciple of the God of the Bible? We're told in Luke 2:52 that Jesus *grew* in wisdom (mentally), in stature (physically), and in favour with God (spiritually) and men (socially). So, by modelling the Master, maturing followers will grow into well-rounded disciples—not just physically and spiritually but also mentally by developing an innocent shrewdness (Matthew 10:16) and socially by becoming true to themselves and at peace with others (Mark 9:50). Yancey writes, "We are not put on earth merely to satisfy our desires, to pursue life, liberty, and happiness. We are here to be changed, to be made more like God in order to prepare us for a lifetime with him" (*Where Is God When It Hurts*, 95).

The Bible tells us that:

1. Disciples will be tested (Job 1:6–42:6; Proverbs 3:11–12, 17:3, 24:10; Matthew 10:16; John 15:1-8; James 1:2–4, 12).

2. Disciples will have the love of God as their priority (Luke 16:10–15).

3. Disciples will make the discipline of the cross their way of life (Matthew 7:13–14, 11:28–30, 16:24–27; Hebrews 12:4–11).

4. Disciples will be stewards of what they possess—they will come to see themselves and everything they own as belonging to God (Psalm 24:1, Philippians 3:7–8).

5. Disciples will have lives that are a testimony to others (Matthew 5:13–16; John 8:31–32, 34–36).

6. Disciples will grow spiritually (Luke 13:20–21, Romans 12:1–2, Philippians 3:12–14).

One additional quality that I would add is *personal integrity.* There will be no falseness or wavering in disciples, no matter what the cost. Job was a person of strong personal integrity (Job 27:5-6) and, on one occasion, Paul rebuked Peter for his *lack* of personal integrity (Galatians 2:11–14). This characteristic is wonderfully illustrated in the portrayal by Paul Scofield of Sir Thomas More in the film *A Man for All Seasons.*

Let's look at what some more recent disciples have said about the process of discipleship. In *Mere Christianity*, C. S. Lewis shares these helpful insights:

> That is why we must not be surprised if we are in for a rough time. When a man turns to Christ and seems to be getting on pretty well (in the sense that some of his bad habits are now corrected), he often feels that it would now be natural if things went fairly smoothly. When troubles come along—illnesses, money troubles, new kinds of temptation—he is disappointed. These things, he feels, might have been necessary to rouse him and make him repent in his bad old days; but why now? Because God is forcing him on, or up, to a higher level: putting him into situations where he will have to be very much braver, or more patient, or more loving, than he ever dreamed of being before. It seems to us all unnecessary: but that is because we

> have not the slightest notion of the tremendous thing He means to make of us (171–2).

In *The Pursuit of God*, A. W. Tozer notes,

> Our pursuit of God is successful just because He is forever seeking to manifest Himself to us. . . .Of course, the will of God is the same for all. He has no favorites. . . . All He has done for any of His children He will do for all of His children. . . . Pick at random a score of great saints. . . . You will be struck instantly with the fact that the saints were not alike. . . . The differences are as wide as human life itself–differences of race, nationality, education, temperament, habit and personal qualities. Yet they all walked, each in his day, upon a high road of spiritual living far above the common way. Their differences must have been incidental and in the eyes of God of no significance. In some vital quality they must have been alike. What was it? I venture to suggest that the one vital quality which they had in common was spiritual receptivity. . . . They differed from the average person in that when they felt the inward longing they did something about it. They acquired the lifelong habit of spiritual response. They were not disobedient to the heavenly vision (65–67).

They followed the "still small voice" leading of God the Holy Spirit.

In the King James translation of Psalm 4:1, King David says that God "enlarged me when I was in distress." In other words, he grew in his faith through his times of trouble. *No* experience is wasted if you walk with God! And you will continue to grow during your entire walk with God if you follow His lead and His ways.

PBPGINFWMY, the first letters abbreviating the words of a slogan that I learned from a Bill Gothard seminar I attended when fairly new in the faith, captures the idea of spiritual growing well: "Please Be Patient—God Is Not Finished With Me Yet." If you cooperate with Him, God will work on making you the best that you can be for your *entire* life! There is no retirement with God! Now, I'm not saying if you become a follower of God, you'll have to keep doing your present job till you die. You *can* retire from that job. What I am saying, though, is that God will *always* have something helpful or useful for you to do—He'll *never* discard you or toss you aside. God will *always* want you working in a way that benefits Him, yourself, and others!

One Final Note on Love

The type of love emphasized in this chapter is *agape* or unconditional love. The Bible also speaks of other kinds of love: *eros* or erotic/sexual love, *phileo* or friendship love, and *storge* or the love one has for family members. The typical relationship in the world is the *marketplace* relationship: you do for me and I'll do for you, or "you scratch my back and I'll scratch yours." Giving—or receiving—unconditional love is a *wonderfully freeing experience.* It means doing for others without expecting *anything* in return; with *no* strings attached, with not even a "thank you" expected. And that's how God loves *you*!

6 A LIFE OBSERVED

Contents

Develop Perspective on the Life You've Lived

Before reading this chapter on "A Life Lived," first bring the perspective of your *own* life to the topic of by answering the following questions:

1. What are some of the childhood issues you faced growing up that you've had to overcome? How did you work on those issues?
2. What effect have those childhood issues had on you as an adult?
3. What are some of the big challenges you've faced as an adult? (e.g., illness, job loss, divorce, death of a family member, etc.)
4. What or who have been the most helpful influences to you in dealing with your childhood issues and your adult challenges?
5. What is your personal testimony about your walk with God? What role has God played in your life? What role does He play on a day-to-day basis in your life?
6. If you were to die today and the people who know you were to chisel their thoughts of you on your tombstone, what might they say? What would you *want* to have said about you on your tombstone? Is there a difference between these two sets of messages? If so, what are you going to do about it?
7. Do you think either an exercise to help you get rid of resentment or an exercise to help you receive healing could be useful to you? Why or why not?
8. Has anything you've been told about the healing profession in church confused you or turned you off? Explain. (e.g., were you told that Christians don't need psychology

or counsellors—they only need the Holy Spirit in order to be healed?)

Overview of the Chapter

In this chapter, I examine my life using two frames of reference. The first is my "Experience, Strength and Hope," the standard format for those in any of the Twelve Step Recovery movements. I've used some of Erikson's developmental insights to organize the data in this section. I also incorporate the useful insights described by Black and Drozd as "signposts on the spiral path" to supplement Erikson, and I reference Cermak's helpful analysis of the symptoms of Post Traumatic Stress Disorder, or PTSD.[18]

The second frame of reference is my "personal testimony," complete with Scripture references, a form familiar to evangelical Christians. The reader will note the life experiences are the same as in the first section, but covered from a different explanatory perspective.

In the third section, I describe an approach that can helpful in furthering healing.

Introduction

Chapters 2–5 provided an introduction to my personal history and the recovery movement. This chapter, using my personal history as a case study, expands upon the material covered in those prior chapters. My life is traced from its beginnings to the present day.

In my Recovery Journey, I introduce many new concepts for understanding and examining one's life. My hope is that the reader can make the connection between these concepts and his or her own life. When I first entered the "adult child" recovery movement, I was sure my pain was unique. Soon after entering, I found out that my pain was not unique; many others had similar experiences. These are my brothers and sisters in recovery. My

[18] I have also included a fairy tale "in recovery mode" in Appendix 1.

hope is that my story will reach some individuals *isolated* in their pain—from others and from *themselves*—and encourage them to take that first courageous step to begin their own journey of healing

In the second section, which features the highlights of my personal testimony not already given in the earlier chapters, my life and Scriptures relevant to viewing one's life are both in focus. Again, my hope is that the reader is able to see the connection between these experiences, Scripture, and his or her own life; learn for themselves that "*God loves me*"; and join the world-wide fellowship of loving believers.

Finally, the third section describes an approach that I often use to facilitate my own healing. The healing approach I use is explained in enough detail that readers may be encouraged to try it for themselves. That is my hope for those who have this need.

The Experience of a Journey of Recovery

1. Basic Trust vs. Basic Mistrust

Let me begin this section by citing from Erikson's *Childhood and Society*, where he identifies the first of the eight developmental stages (synopsised by Black and Drozd on pages 48–49 of *The Missing Pieces)*. Erikson labels the first stage faced by the new human as "Basic Trust vs. Basic Mistrust."

> But even under the most favourable circumstances, this stage seems to introduce into psychic . . . a sense of inner division and universal nostalgia for a paradise forfeited [life in the womb]. It is against this powerful combination of a sense of having been deprived, of having been divided, and of having been abandoned—that basic trust must maintain itself throughout life (250).

I would maintain that if the newborn has a nostalgia for life in the womb, that presupposes a benign uterine environment and, if this is not the case, then basic trust is further compromised and basic mistrust is correspondingly enhanced. This was the situation in my case, as my story below illustrates.

Childhood Impact

When I was around ten, my mother told me that she had attempted in some way to have an abortion when she was pregnant with me because her relationship with her husband, my father, was so poor. Her water broke while my parents were in a cinema watching a movie, so they had to rush to the hospital. She let me know that this was before she knew and loved me, so it was "nothing personal." There is apparently a biochemical secretion the foetus can activate to speed up their birth and I believe that I activated this biochemical and was born more than two months premature at a weight of just under two lbs. When my paternal grandmother first saw me, I was so small and jaundiced that she stated, "That's not going to live." I then spent the next month or two in a hospital incubator getting my weight "up to snuff." During that time, my mother came to breastfeed me at the hospital; also, she expressed her breast milk and then brought it to the hospital for the nurses to use in bottle-feeding me when she wouldn't be there. As a preschooler, I have fond memories of my mother rocking me to sleep for my afternoon nap while crooning a lullaby.

I imagine the "abandonment" after birth would have contributed negatively, and the "loving rocking" positively, to my "Basic Trust vs. Basic Mistrust".

From my earliest recollections, my parents' relationship was poor. I remember their fights—verbal, not physical—with words so laden with bitter emotion they terrified me. I could not believe that they would stay together after saying such mean things to each other, which meant that I would be abandoned and I had nowhere else to go! While a preschooler, when these emotional assaults happened, I would run to my bed—which was in my parents' bedroom—and, through a compulsive routine, it became an imaginary spaceship that whisked me away from there.

As I got older, I used a different way to cope with their word-based fisticuffs. I became hyper-vigilant or acutely sensitive to the beginnings of a verbal parental storm and would do whatever I could to distract them whenever I sensed a storm brewing. I would ask questions, tell stories, make comments, relate jokes, etc.—any people-pleasing thing I could do—to keep them from beginning a verbal fight. This gave me a sense of control, which, though false, I found reassuring. To maintain this sense of control, it was essential that I ignore my own feelings. If I was going to pay attention to what was going on with them, I couldn't afford to focus on what was going on inside of me. As a child, I had no close friends.

Adult Impact

As a young adult, I frequently isolated myself and had no close friends—I did not attempt to develop close friendships until I was in my fifties, no doubt the result of Basic Mistrust. However, when isolating, one can get away from others and from situations, but one cannot get away from oneself!

I married twice and both times was able to successfully replicate the conditions of my parents' home, for the reasons noted in chapter 2. I developed "instant pseudo-intimacy" with both wives. Before I left my parents' home, I was living with the woman who would become my first wife, and before our divorce was finalized, I was living with the woman who would become my second wife—the result of the powerful effects both of a fear of abandonment and of a need to resolve the effects of my childhood experience of parental emotional unavailability and emotional abuse. The manner in which both relationships began and then evolved ensured there would be no intimacy—I was afraid of intimacy and my wives did not provide it.

2. Autonomy vs. Shame and Doubt

According to Erikson,

> Outer control at this stage ... must be firmly reassuring [for autonomy to successfully develop].... For if denied the gradual and well-guided experience of the autonomy of free choice (or if, indeed, weakened by an initial loss of trust) the child will turn against himself.... He will overmanipulate himself, he will develop a precocious conscience.... [H]e will become obsessed by his own repetitiveness.... [H]e then learns to repossess the environment and to gain power by stubborn and minute control.... Shame is early expressed in an impulse to . . . sink, right then and there, into the ground . . . Doubt is the brother of shame.... From . . . a sense of loss of self-control and of foreign overcontrol comes a lasting propensity for doubt and shame (252–254).

In addition, Bly comments in *Iron John* that,

> Each child lives deep inside his or her own psychic house, or soul castle, and the child deserves the right of sovereignty inside that house. Whenever a parent ignores the child's sovereignty, and invades, the child feels not only anger, but shame. The child concludes that if it has no sovereignty, it must be worthless (147).

Childhood Impact

From this point on in my development as a child, any attempts at my emotional self-expression were either punished with expressions of anger or shamed with expressions of fear and sadness. My methods of dealing with my parents' fights were escape and control. And, somewhere inside, I came to believe that I was the cause of my parents' fighting, so obviously, I should be able to control it. The belief that they fought because of me, coupled with my failures in controlling their fighting, I'm sure helped to convince me that I must be inherently flawed, contributing to a sense of shame. If I was not flawed and inherently inferior, my parents wouldn't fight!

Adult Impact

As an adult, I have engaged in compulsive behaviours such as drinking, eating, and working as a way of masking and avoiding having to deal with my painful emotions. I was a people-pleaser, caretaker and rescuer in my relationships as a way of dealing with my abandonment fears. I chose as partners women I felt I could rescue, believing they would love me out of gratitude, and I was careful as a consultant, especially early on, to say things in a manner not upsetting to clients (people-pleasing).

3. Initiative vs. Guilt

Erikson says that, during this period,

> . . . the child is at no time more ready to learn quickly and avidly, to become bigger in the sense of sharing obligations and performance than during this period of his development. He is eager and able to make things cooperatively . . . with other children . . . and . . . teachers. He remains, of course, identified with the parent of the same sex . . . (258).

Childhood Impact

I remember playing cooperatively with neighbourhood children at home and outside as a preschooler and in kindergarten with classmates; teachers found me cooperative. I have fond memories of my father taking me to a couple of train stations to watch the big steam engines. We'd always have a treat afterwards—ice cream at one station and chewing gum at the other. One Christmas, I received as a gift a wooden horse and wagon and I proudly removed the nails from it so that my father could use them for "something useful." In high school, my initiative and desire to innovate often overshadowed my desire to cooperate with teachers.

My mother observed that I was a shy child and so enrolled me in dramatic/acting lessons which involved my performing on stage before a public that footlights hid from me. Those acting lessons helped me to "come out of myself."

As a preschooler, I got lost once. I became separated from my parents—lost in my mind—after a semi-professional softball game. My parents watched the game, which was at a neighbourhood park, while I played in the sandbox that was adjacent to the ball diamond. When the crowd stood up and started to leave after the game had ended, I could no longer see my parents, got scared, and started crying. A kindly man with two children and a wife in tow saw my plight, assured me that my parents would find me, and then bought me a chocolate ice cream cone. We then started slowly walking on the path toward my home. My worried parents soon caught up with us and thanked the family.

Adult Impact

As a worker, I was cooperative with my peers and, initially in my working career, with my supervisors. In later years, initiative often superseded cooperation with those in charge.

In my twenties, I enrolled in a ten-week Christopher's Public Speaking Course. I was so nervous speaking before my peer classmates for the three minute period we all spoke each week that, for the first six weeks, my knees knocked. After that, I lost my "stage fright" and enjoyed the experience.

Ice cream and chocolate remained my "comfort foods" of choice, my compulsive eating favourites, until I was in my late sixties.

4. Industry vs. Inferiority

As Erikson notes at this stage, the child

> . . . develops a sense of industry—i.e., he adjusts himself to . . . the tool world. . . . To bring a productive situation to completion is an aim which gradually supersedes the whims and

wishes of play. . . .[T]he work principle . . . teaches him the pleasure of work completion by steady attention and persevering diligence. . . . School seems to be a culture all by itself, with its own goals and limits, its achievements and disappointments. The child's danger, at this stage, lies in a sense of inadequacy and inferiority. . . . [T]his is socially a most decisive stage: since industry involves doing things beside and with others (259–260).

Childhood Impact

In elementary school, I did well—I was a conscientious student. I saw education as the avenue to a successful career in adulthood. I also had many school chums. It was during this stage that my mother orchestrated an event that effectively ended my relationship with my father until I was in my mid-thirties.

It was a lovely summer Saturday morning when I was about ten years old. My father and I were working together making a model airplane on the kitchen table. All of a sudden, my mother came into the kitchen, said something like, "It's too nice a day to be inside; don't waste your time on that," and tried to smash the plane. My father held it away from her, but I smashed it and then went outside to play. In that event, I had shattered not only the plane but my relationship with my father. I had devastated my father in order to please my mother. From that point on in my childhood, I no longer had an intimate relationship with my father—all the intimacy I had from then on was with my mother. Bly notes in Iron John that "To be without a supportive father is for a man an alternative phrase for 'to be in shame'"(198).

Adult Impact

I was a competent and creative worker. Competence was my way of overcoming my felt inferiority. If I was a better worker than others, this would allow me to compensate for what I *knew* was an inferiority inherent in my being. I'm confident that the "airplane incident" unconsciously reduced my trust level for women. It also led to my getting involved in the North American Men's Movement—The ManKind Project—for a brief period of time when I was in my late sixties since I had lost my father's influence at too young an age.

5. Identity vs. Role Confusion

According to Erikson:

> The integration now taking place in the form of ego identity is ... the accrued experience of the ego's ability to integrate all identifications. . . . The danger of this stage is role confusion. Where this is based on a strong previous doubt as to one's . . . identity, delinquent . . . episodes are not uncommon. . . . In most instances . . . it is the inability to settle on an occupational identity which disturbs young people (261–262).

Childhood Impact

I maintained the diverse and disparate aspects of my world through compartmentalization. Everybody and everything had their own "box." I always knew my job future, though that future job often changed. My initial career choices were driving—a variety of vehicles—followed by becoming a garbage collector. But the choice that I made at age ten, a choice which stayed with me until I was a second year university student, was to become an MD. This choice was occasioned by my receiving a "Dr. UB Well" play medical kit from my parents for Christmas that year; it was the first career choice I made that truly pleased them. I began summer vacation jobs at age fourteen.

My brush with delinquency occurred when I was thirteen or fourteen and involved wandering the local train yards with a couple of school chums. One of my chums threw a green tomato through the window of a street car whose route went through the train yard. The police caught us and individually brought us home. The look on my father's face when he saw me at the door of our apartment in the company of a police officer said that he foresaw a criminal career for me. I never again played with those two school chums.

Adult Impact

I worked hard—and successfully—at developing superior competence in every job I ever had. I also became a volunteer at a prison.

6. Intimacy vs. Isolation

Erikson states,

> The young adult, emerging from the search for an insistence on identity, is eager and willing to fuse his identity with that of others. He is ready for intimacy . . . even though [it] may call for significant sacrifices and compromises. . . . The counterpart of intimacy is distantation: the readiness to isolate and, if necessary, to destroy those forces and people whose essence seems dangerous to one's own. . . . The danger of this stage is isolation, that is the avoidance of contacts which commit to intimacy (263–266).

Childhood Antecedents

Through adolescence I feared abandonment, so I desperately sought intimacy but lacked the emotional awareness of self and the ability to trust others sufficiently to be intimate. This attitude I carried into adulthood.

Adult Evolution

I chose women with whom I could have "instant pseudo-emotional intimacy" but once achieved, however briefly, I would quickly sabotage it, ensuring that I remained an emotional isolate.

I believe that the length of time that I was emotionally isolated was exacerbated by my lifelong living arrangements. I lived at home when I first attended university because it made economic sense. The university was in the same city and living at home was cheaper than living in residence or off-campus. When I moved away to go to my first post-graduate university, I was married. And before we divorced, I was living with the woman who became my second wife. I did not live on my own, except for temporary periods, until I was sixty-five years old!

I believe that living alone greatly enhances maturation and individuation. Parents, help your children grow up! Help them live on their own away from you before they marry. Let them find out who they are and the kind of people that they like and dislike. Be courageous and unconditionally loving parents! As Bly states in Iron John, "If a man or woman has . . . lived in any form of a 'dysfunctional family', he or she will need sooner or later a 'heaven-haven'. . . . [E]ach of us needs it. . . . [It] is a shelter from the world, and a place to recover from broken trust" (129).

7. Generativity vs. Stagnation

Erikson maintains:

> Generativity . . . is primarily the concern in establishing and guiding the next generation. . . . [T]he concept generativity is meant to include such more popular synonyms as *productivity* and *creativity*, which, however, cannot replace it. . . . Where such enrichment fails altogether, regression to an obsessive need for pseudo-intimacy takes place, often with a pervading sense of stagnation and personal impoverishment (267).

Childhood Antecedents

At the earliest stages, I learned that the only safe way to ensure the desired outcome in relationship development is to maintain control. Things will go wrong if I'm not in control.

Adult Evolution

I was productive and creative in the task/work domain. My approach to guiding my children was through control—an approach which they generally resisted. The older and more independent they got, the more "pseudo" my intimacy became. It was not until they were adults that I began to achieve a genuine intimacy with them. I never reached this stage with my wives.

8. Ego Integrity vs. Despair

Erikson concludes that:

> Only in him who in some way has taken care of things and people and has adapted himself to the triumphs and disappointments adherent to being, the originator of others or the generator of products and ideas—only in him may gradually ripen the fruit of these seven [previous] stages. . . . It is the acceptance of one's one and only life cycle as something that had to be and that, by necessity, permitted of no substitutions: it thus means a new, a different love of one's parents. . . . The lack or loss of this accrued ego integration [despair] is signified by fear of death: the one and only life cycle is not accepted as the ultimate of life. . . . Ego integrity, therefore, implies an emotional integration. . . . [H]ealthy children will not fear life if their elders have integrity enough not to fear death (268–269).

In *Death of a Salesman*, at the end of his life Willy Loman archetypifies "despair."

This chapter is a description of emotional integration in my own life. My hope is that it will facilitate the emotional integration of the lives of others, including my children's, who have been affected by similar developmental issues.

Black and Drozd describe steps that I believe are important to the achievement of ego integrity. They call them the eight "signposts on the spiral path" (161–185). They are, in order:

1. Denial: A lack of readiness to have awareness of one's issues.
2. Identification: What's not working in one's life/the first step in the twelve step program.
3. Remembering: aspects of your painful past.
4. Grief: the emotions—anger/rage. sadness/depression, shame, etc. associated with *remembering* your past.
5. Letting Go: of your past.
6. Acceptance: of your past.
7. Learning New Skills: in thinking, feeling, and behaving.
8. Genesis: A new beginning or re-genesis/reintegration around the new healed self.

Childhood Antecedents

My major emotional life work was to overcome the Basic Mistrust of my origins.

Adult Evolution

At forty, I gained faith in a Personal God. In my early fifties, I accepted my need for healing and began my redevelopment. My healing began initially with the aid of therapists and self-healing literature and then increasingly involved twelve step recovery groups, mostly Adult Children of Alcoholics and Al-Anon. But through it all, the active intervention of God, my Higher Power, was always there.

My "spiral path" evolution

1. Denial

Up until my early fifties, my view was that I'd had a normal childhood and that overly strong emotional expression was something to be avoided. My wife and children had issues, but not me.

Two terms important to understanding dysfunctional behaviour are "acting out" and "denial." Behaviour that is motivated by unresolved personal psychological issues is called "acting-out." If the acting-out is directed against oneself, it is self-abuse—for instance, alcoholism or drug abuse. Alternatively, if the acting-out is directed against others, it is anti-social. Criminal behaviour is serious acting-out behaviour directed against others. I acted-out against myself and my family.

"Denial" is usually seen in negative terms, which is a misconception. "Denial" is the psyche's way of saying to a person: "You're not ready to deal with this pain yet." The child uses compulsive behaviours to "magically" achieve the safety of denial. Addictions are adult compulsive behaviours. As Tolle notes in *The Power of Now*:

> Every addiction arises from an unconscious refusal to face and move through your own pain. Every addiction starts with pain and ends with pain. Whatever the substance you are addicted to—alcohol, food, legal or illegal drugs, or a person—you are using something or somebody to cover up your pain (152).

I believe that the *cause* of denial is the inability of the person to deal with and process the trauma they are experiencing; the only alternative to experiencing the pain and terror they are facing that is open to them is denial. Cermak, in *A Time to Heal*, describes surviving being brought up in a dysfunctional home as equivalent to the Post Traumatic Stress Disorder (PTSD) of war vets. He says, "PTSD develops when a person's normal coping mechanisms are confronted with abnormal levels of stress, overwhelming that person's ability to break the stress down into digestible bites" (77). Cermak describes the four symptoms of PTSD:

i. **Re-experiencing the Trauma**: immediate intense emotion, fear response to someone's anger or the prospect of losing a relationship, extreme defensiveness when criticized, and startle responses to small events that preceded arguments when you were a youngster (87-88).

ii. **Psychic Numbing**: having no feelings during times of stress, being "confused" instead of having feelings, just having a lump in your throat instead of allowing feelings to emerge, and fearing that feelings will overwhelm you if they begin to be shown (92). I would add "Minimizing feeling physical pain" to that list.

iii. **Hypervigilance**: constantly checking that others have done their jobs correctly, assuming anything that goes wrong is the first sign of catastrophe, keeping lists in your head of all the things that have to be done before you can relax, and constantly feeling there is something that you ought to be doing (98–99).

iv. **Survivor Guilt**: feeling callous if you don't help people who say they need you—even if they've created their own problems, restraining yourself from feeling real joy, finding some way that you might be responsible for other people's unhappiness or misfortune, and refusing to leave relationships and situations that are unhealthy for you in order to avoid feeling guilty (102).

Loss of family can also lead to PTSD, as Adam Sandler portrays in the film *Reign Over Me*, as Hammer describes in the tragic case of "street person" David White, and in some "street people" I've met—theirs is the "crushed spirit" of Proverbs 18:14.

The article "Silencing of the Lambs" in the *Economist* suggests that childhood abuse may even change the way genes work and increase suicidal tendencies.

In chapter 3, I spoke of getting rid of my longstanding anxiety with not being late and about releasing my lifetime of resentment. In the next section on my personal testimony, I describe dealing with my lifelong co-dependency and also explain arriving at the conclusion that my two marriages were over. I believe that I remained in denial all those years because I wasn't ready to deal with the issues *underlying* my denial.

2. Identification and 3. Remembering

In my early fifties, I began coming out of denial and remembering aspects of my past. It began with becoming aware that there were things going on inside me that I didn't understand but needed to. The issues that for me were critical to deal with were:

a. ***Isolation and Mistrust***. This was my first approach to dealing with the terror that was my home. Both as a child and as an adult, my isolation typically took on the form of emotional absence—I would be safe if I wasn't there emotionally or didn't get too close emotionally to others. I continued to isolate myself and remained emotionally unavailable for most of my life.

   My mother mistrusted both my father and her first husband, whom she believed were unfaithful to her. My father had only work acquaintances as an adult, no friends.

b. ***Control***. This was my second approach to dealing with an unsafe world, an approach which was more appealing than isolating since it meant that I could impact my world in a way that seemed to make it "safer." During my years as a student in school, my attempts at social control, especially with my parents, consisted mainly of distracting them so they wouldn't fight. As an adult, I got good at people-pleasing, caretaking, and rescuing.

c. ***Avoidance of Feelings***. Control of others was impossible if I was going to be crippled by my own fear and sadness—my anger was an unsafe emotion for me as a child. The only safe feeling for me then was "numb." As an adult, I added "anger" to my repertoire of safe emotions. And "anger," as I learned later in "Anger Management" sessions, is a mask emotion, typically masking "fear" or "sadness."

I borrowed many of my parents' ways of avoiding feelings.

My mother used alcohol to dull her pain. She was also a compulsive eater. As I got older, I needed the help of alcohol to maintain numbness, and I still have to work on my compulsive eating tendencies.

My father was a gambling addict. He told me that he twice bet a year's salary on a horse race and then, when he realized what a fool he was to risk money he could not afford to lose, he converted himself into a two-dollar bettor. He was also a workaholic and a perfectionist. I "gambled"—stock trading is gambling—with my retirement savings and lost more than half before I saw the insanity of my ways and converted myself into an investor. Let me explain the difference. Investing involves putting money in some undervalued *asset*, whereas gambling involves putting money on the *behaviour* of the asset. If I buy a horse that I believe can win a significant number of races, I'm *investing* in a speculative asset; however, if I bet on a horse, I'm *gambling* that the horse will finish first, second, or third in a race. If I buy a penny stock that I believe is undervalued because it owns property that may contain significant natural resources, I'm *investing* in a speculative asset; if I buy a stock whose price I believe will move up for "*technical*" reasons, such as "cup and handle" or "double bottom," I'm *gambling* on the behaviour of the stock price.

I am still a workaholic. An interesting glimpse into my father's perfectionism as it affected me involved my Grade Six elementary school report card, where all my academic subjects except one were graded "excellent" and that one was graded "very good." My father didn't compliment me on the report but instead asked me why the "very good" wasn't an "excellent." When I was in my thirties, after our relationship was being re-established, I asked him about it. His answer was that complimenting me might have led me to "slack off."

4. Grief, 5. Letting Go, and 6. Acceptance

During my recovery years, as I became aware of my past I experienced strong emotions—mostly sadness and anger. The biggest emotional events that I dealt with were my mother's idea of aborting me, my parents' fighting, and the "plane-smashing" incident orchestrated by my mother.

7. Learning New Skills

The most important value of the pain of my past was how it served as an impetus to personal growth. During my early recovery years, I took a course in learning how to feel one's feelings. I remember the first time I really felt fear—it felt like waves of emotion flowing through me.

Another skill I learned was to be honest about my feelings and views with others no matter what the effect on those others might be. If others didn't like my views or feelings, that was their problem, not mine. I learned this skill through hearing others share their experiences, and me sharing mine, at twelve step meetings.

Finally, the last important skill that I learned was to love myself—and for me it was a skill. I say "skill" because loving myself was something I had to *learn* to do and not an inherent ability that I had. Essential to learning this was the experience of realizing that God loved me just as I was. As stated earlier, the logic that my standards shouldn't be higher than God's hit me: if God could love me just as I was, then surely I could learn to love myself that way as well. I began with the twelve step slogans "Fake it till you make it" or "Act as if" you *do* love yourself—do loving things, do what's best for yourself, even if you don't feel like it. And gradually, as I learned to do this for myself, I became able to do it for others. I learned to love others unconditionally, not in a co-dependent manner but with no strings attached. What a wonderfully freeing experience it was when I started loving others unconditionally!

8. Genesis

For me, "genesis" occurred in achieving "ego integrity" which, as noted above, happened in my late sixties. It has enabled me to embrace all of my life and be grateful for it. As my Al-Anon sponsor, Robbie R., helped me understand, *all* the experiences of my life—pleasant and unpleasant—have made me who I am today, and for that I am truly grateful. The writing of this book is for me an "ego integrity" project. While "pain" was the catalyst for my personal growth, "happiness" has been the catalyst underlying my productivity, including the writing of this book.

A Personal Testimony: Nuggets Along My Way

GOD

1. In My Beginning

I didn't have any conscious awareness of God in my early life, but Psalm 139 assures me that He was there. As a child, I went to St. Luke's United Church because their minister was the first person of a religious persuasion to visit my parents before I was born and they believed that going to church would be a good thing for me to do. My dad was brought up Anglican, my mom Roman Catholic, and they married in the United, but neither went to church, except for funerals and weddings, all the years that I knew them. The benefit that I obtained from going to church, besides fooling around with my pals in Sunday school and the bottle of pop afterwards (bought with half of the collection money my parents had given me), was an appreciation of the message in some of the hymns—especially "Jesus Loves Me"—and a fascination with some of the stories the missionaries told, like the Central American family for whom their annual treat was a *loaf of bread* bought from a store at Christmastime. I think the hymns and the missionary stories stirred up an interest in God for me. As Psalm 19:7–10 states, the things of God stir the soul.

Looking back today, I believe that God sustained me from conception through the difficult early months after my birth, and I believe He has watched over me ever since (Psalm 22:9–11, 139:13–16).

2. My Conversion Process

a. A Personal God

As described in chapter 4, my first conscious awareness of God came when I was a university student at McGill. At the time, I believed in God as Creator of the Universe but not as an active participant in its affairs. In my mind, God had opted for retirement after creation and left the operation of the Universe to Science, which had the potential to answer *all* questions. This meant that humans were biological machines—wonderful machines, but still just machines! At the same time, I was in love with a young French Roman Catholic woman. So there I was, in love and believing that people are machines. Then, one day during my second year at McGill as I was walking along Sherbrooke street in front of the university, I heard what I thought was a voice. The voice said, "Machines can't love." I was so startled that I looked all around to discover who had spoken to me, but no-one was there. I then came to the conclusion that God had "spoken" to me—as I now understand it, He put that thought in my mind. This was my first conscious awareness of God being actively involved in my personal world. As a result, I became interested in finding out more about Him and His ways.

b. The Roman Road

Because she was a good Catholic, part of the "deal" for me, a Protestant, dating this young French woman, was that I had to take instruction in her faith. So, once a week, I met for an hour or so with a priest, himself an English convert from Anglicanism, to learn about Roman Catholicism. I felt this was a small price to pay for dating a girl I loved and, when I began, that was the only reason that I was doing it. However, after I heard from God, I had a sincere interest in finding out all I could. Later, I converted to the Roman faith and was confirmed by Paul-Emile Cardinal Leger.

I remained a Roman Catholic for ten years. There were two main reasons that I abandoned that persuasion: 1. I divorced my first wife and remarried without an annulment, giving me the permanent status of "bad catholic," and 2. I discovered that no matter how hard or how sincerely I tried, I could never be good enough to save myself. I kept confessing the same sins (lost my temper, for instance) every week in my sessions in the confessional. I was unable to earn my way to heaven. In spite of my imperfections, I was on the "salvation road," as 1 Corinthians 1:18 describes, and so received God's protection, as Psalm 91:14–16 so beautifully promises: "'Because he loves me,' says the Lord, 'I will rescue him; I will protect him, for he acknowledges my name. He will call upon me, and I will answer him; I will be with him in trouble, I will deliver him and honor him. With long life will I satisfy him and show him my salvation.'" All of these promises have come true in my life!

c. A Man Called John

When I first met John I was in bad shape. I was an alcoholic consuming 66 oz of Captain Morgan's Black Label Rum from Thursday to Sunday (I drank it with Diet Pepsi because "you've got to watch the calories"). Most Monday mornings at work I could smell and taste the un-metabolized liquor on my breath. In AA terms, "I was powerless over alcohol and my life had become unmanageable": my second marriage and my job at a large multinational company, which provided enough money to maintain ownership of our home, were both in jeopardy. John talked about "a personal relationship with Jesus" and being "born again." Without fully understanding what I was doing, I decided to "give it a shot." I was fearful because I saw John as a fanatic and didn't want to become like him; I also thought that becoming a Christian was the end of fun in my life—"sackcloth and ashes time"—but I was also powerless over alcohol and my life had become unmanageable.

So, in spite of my fears, on Saturday morning, December 17, 1978—one day before my fortieth birthday—I knelt beside my bed and asked Jesus to come into my life. This was not a great act of faith, but rather, an act of desperation. My life was such a mess that I figured I had nothing to lose. I was ready to find refuge in God (Psalm 62:8, 91:2). I felt no different immediately afterward, so wasn't sure if I'd "done it right." The first people I shared it with, after my wife, were our Pastor Jim Cantelon and his wife, who "just happened" to visit us that day.

After they left, just before supper, when I'd normally start drinking that day's 16 oz. of Captain Morgan's, I realized a miracle had occurred in my life—I *didn't want* to drink. This wasn't "mind over matter" or "willpower": the *desire* to drink had been taken away from me by God! I believe that this was a gracious sign from God to show me that my salvation by grace had "taken." I was really reborn, a sinner saved by the grace of God from hell (Psalm 30:3; 116:1, 4, 8). Life for me truly began again at forty; I was no longer a prodigal coming home but was now a fully adopted child of God (Galatians 4:7, Ephesians 1:5)!

3. The Development of My Relationship with God

a. The First Ten or so Years

It had been a long time since I'd been "religious," so I figured I "owed God big time," and needed to make up for lost time. I couldn't accept salvation by grace, so I had to earn it. I became a "Pharisee" for the ungracious God I believed in, in spite of the grace He'd shown me in my salvation experience. I went to church every Sunday, tithed, went to most church meetings, ushered, counted offerings, taught Sunday school, became a deacon, and did other jobs as requested.

Now, let me be quick to add that these can all be good things to do. The problem was with my motivation: these things were being done because I *had to*—I felt I owed so much to God for 40 years of neglect. I also had to tightly control my home so my family wouldn't add more to my debt load with God. I believe most of the church people who knew me then saw me as a "good Christian," but truthfully, I was living the life of a legalistic Christian and not a gracious one. And just as I'd discovered that perfection was not possible as a Catholic, I now learned that it was also not possible as a born-again Christian. In spite of my attitude, God favoured me with His grace from the beginning. However, it took me over ten years to begin accepting that His love was unconditional.

God often "spoke" to me by putting thoughts in my head during that first ten years. I described some of them earlier in chapter 3.

b. *Retirement, Anger, Communion and Recovery*

On June 30, 1989, at age fifty, I got to retire from the large multinational company where I had been employed with an enhanced pension immediately available and a consulting contract starting the next day. I now believe that this was arranged because God knew I needed a lot of healing. The beginning of my healing, as described in chapter 5, was triggered soon after that retirement by my angry reaction to my innocently sleeping wife. God showed me that there were things going on inside me that I didn't understand but desperately needed to address (Nahum 1:7).

Now aware that I needed help, I went to see a counsellor. This was the beginning of my journey of recovery. Over time, I saw several counsellors, all of whom helped me gain insight into myself. With a counsellor, however, it is not a peer relationship but rather a relationship with an authority figure: the counsellor has more knowledge/insight than you and gets paid for their services. The Twelve Step Movement, on the other hand, is based on peer relationships. The first group I joined was Overeaters Anonymous (OA), because I often ate compulsively. This was my beginning in the recovery movement.

Soon after I joined OA, I attended a seminar in Toronto called "Communion with God" taught by Mark Virkler. There I learned to quiet myself and listen for God's "voice"—not actually an audible voice but thoughts put in my head, much as had happened to me in Montreal around thirty years prior. Through this experience over the years, I have learned that God loves me unconditionally. This has enabled me to gradually love myself unconditionally since I can't be so arrogant or proud to believe that my standards should be higher than God's! The more I love myself unconditionally, the better able I am to love others unconditionally.

Loving others unconditionally is a very freeing condition—you give with *no strings attached*! *Conditional* loving for me meant giving but expecting something in return; if I gave you something or did something for you, you now *owed* me something! For example, for most of my adult years, I resented people I gave greeting cards to who didn't reciprocate. Today, I give greeting cards because *I want to give them* and, because there are no strings attached, this means I can really *enjoy* giving them. And it isn't just greeting cards; the other *giving* I do is also unconditional.

In the late fall of 1993, my second wife and I separated for incompatibility reasons. I moved from Newmarket to Toronto, desperate to better understand the things going on inside of me. On a cold late autumn Thursday night that felt like winter, I attended my first meeting of Adult Children of Alcoholics (ACA). Where OA had enabled me to deal with my compulsive eating, ACA helped me understand *why* I needed to eat compulsively and many other issues. Unfortunately, ACA, an offshoot of Al-Anon, is not a robust fellowship. So where no ACA group is available, I look for Adult Children Al-Anon groups—even when on vacation in Florida. An "adult child" is a person who is physically and mentally an adult but emotionally still reacts as they did as a child in some situations.

Fuelling my anger was resentment over things that had happened in my past that I had never let go of. With these resentments inside me, when I got angry I greatly overreacted, making "mountains out of molehills." I wasn't reacting to the situation at hand; rather, my reaction was inflamed by the more than seventy-five unhealed resentments that I carried around inside of me.[19] Since then, I still get angry, but it is situational rather than fuelled by resentment that has never been released and forgiven.

c. *Marriage and Divorce*

I have been married twice and divorced twice. It is easiest to think of this is as two failures, but I don't. Instead, I think of it as success! Let me explain. Hendrix, a former Baptist Pastor, as explained earlier, states that we choose the person we marry to enable us to work through the developmental issues we never resolved while growing up in our family of origin home. He further states that if we *fail* to work through those issues, we will repeat them in our next marriage. I experienced my parents' relationship as lacking in intimacy and involving emotional isolation from, and emotionally unavailability to, each other. I also sometimes experienced them as abusive toward me and each other. So I married two women: the first I experienced as emotionally unavailable and overtly abusive, and the second I found to be emotionally unavailable and covertly abusive. I was emotionally unavailable for both of them and, when angry or defensive, was also emotionally abusive.

I divorced my first wife because I could no longer take the abuse. We talked about attempting reconciliation after a year of separation, but she asked me for a divorce less than six months after we'd separated so she could marry her supervisor at work. My ongoing emotional healing during my second marriage led me to discover my need for emotional support and to seek a divorce from my second wife, who was unwilling to work together on our developing a mutually supportive and intimate

---

[19] I also describe this in chapter 3.

relationship. She wouldn't work toward our becoming each other's "best friend," even with counselling assistance. For me to stay in that relationship after I became aware of my need for emotional support and intimacy would have been self-abuse and a lack of self-love.

If I had married the young French Roman Catholic woman, I believe the relationship would have been a happy one, *but I never would have had to deal with my developmental issues*! I needed relationships that would mimic my parents' home situation to be able to grow out of my "adult child hang-ups." It's important to understand that neither of my wives were "bad people." A bad person commits evil acts to deliberately harm another person. My wives behaved in the manner they acquired in their own dysfunctional family of origin homes, just as I did. As I see it, I was an opportunity for them to work on their own unresolved "family of origin" issues. I hope they were able to do that.

One question that may come to mind is, if I was so unhappy, why not have an affair? I can recall three opportunities to have a fling in each of my marriages, but I was never really tempted to cheat on my wives. The reasons I wasn't tempted were: first of all, I knew it was wrong, and secondly, I also understood that an affair would simply make my loneliness worse. Sex without a loving relationship is empty—it is simply "sex" and would have reinforced my loneliness by the absence of an accompanying intimacy. This latter point is well illustrated by the Willy Loman character in *Death of a Salesman*. From Terry Gorski, a recovery counsellor, I learned about the healthy evolution of a relationship, which I described in chapter 2.

4. Retrospective

Genesis 39:1—50:21 shows that God was with Joseph through all of his "dark times." In Genesis 50:20, Joseph tells his brothers that God used the "dark times" for good.

This tells me:

1. *God was with me during the times of darkness in my life.*

2. *God used the times of darkness in my life for a good purpose*, as promised in Romans 8:28.

3. *The darkness will last as long as God needs to accomplish His purpose.* This means as long as you or I fight God and don't surrender, the darkness, and our *suffering*, will continue.

In the twelve step programs, the steps don't begin until we admit our life is unmanageable. Remember, denial tells us we're not ready to deal with an issue. When we're ready to deal with it, we can come out of denial. Also remember that all suffering *handicaps* us in some way, so truthfully, since we all suffer, *we're all handicapped.* Some handicaps are physical, some mental, some emotional, and others spiritual. Some handicaps we are born with, while others we acquire naturally or by accident as we grow up or grow old. Some are not even recognized as handicaps, as noted by Kellogg in *Broken Toys, Broken Dreams*. He states, for instance, the workaholism of the "high achiever" student is seen positively and not as "handicap." By extension, the workaholism of the "Fortune 500" CEO is seen as a fitting price of success and not as a handicap, and the emotional abusiveness of the powerful leader is seen as inherent in the stress, demands, or power of their position.

What is most important with respect to dealing with handicaps is, first of all, to *recognize* them as such and then to *respond* appropriately to them. A couple of good examples are Paul and his "thorn in the flesh" (2 Corinthians 12:7–10) and Joni Eareckson Tada and her quadriplegia. First, each asked God to remove the handicap, and then when it wasn't, they accepted the handicap and got on with the life God had for them. They didn't allow the handicap to cripple them as vibrant, abundant-living human beings!

4. *I will learn more in the dark times than in the times of light in my life.*

5. *Even in the dark times, I was struggling toward the light.*

6. *What we learn in the darkness, we are to share with others when we come out into the light.* Charles Stanley's article, "Brokenness—The Way to Blessing" describes the darkness of brokenness as a way to the light of blessing.

An Approach to Healing

These healing insights come from two sources. The first comes from J. Konrad Stettbacher's *Making Sense of Suffering: The Healing Confrontation with Your Own Past.*[20] The second source also comes from a book: *Why People Don't Heal and How They Can,*[21] written by Caroline Myss.

For me, the most useful section of Stettbacher's book is found in pages 57–69, which I excerpt as follows:

> The four steps are based on our inborn, primal ability to establish relationships to ourselves and the world around us.
>
> The order of the four steps corresponds to the building blocks of our functions as they determine our interactive ability. . . .
>
> In the following overview, the four steps are not described in full detail. They are guidelines and do not pretend to be complete. Each individual will conduct the dialogue with his or her own words. What is crucial, however, is that all four steps be performed in each interaction. . . .
>
> "Success" has been achieved as soon as symptoms disappear. . . .
>
> A written therapy is appropriate when material circumstances make "live" work impossible. Therapy by correspondence is a well-tried method for promoting self-help. Your situation, sensations, feelings, and conclusions can be very precisely formulated in writ-

---

[20] (New York: Meridian, 1993). I learned of his book by reading Alice Miller's *Banished Knowledge*, which I in turn learned of by reading her more famous *The Drama of the Gifted Child.* (See References for details.)
[21] (New York: Harmony Books, 1997).

> ten form, as can your needs and queries. Write as though you were speaking freely, without censorship. The four steps can be checked and supplemented in the act of re-reading what you have written. A therapy based on writing and reflection cannot . . . be a complete substitute . . . for the speaking /feeling part of therapy that completes the . . . interaction."

I found the most helpful notion in Myss's book to be the emphasis on forgiveness as essential to healing, illustrated by a quote from page 18:

> The only way to release the pattern into which we have locked ourselves is to release the weight of the past—to get at the cause of the energy debt we can no longer afford to carry. Forgiveness is one sure way out of debt. Forgiving does not mean saying that what happened to you doesn't matter, or that it is all right for someone to have violated you. It simply means releasing the negative feelings about the event and the person or persons involved. This is clearly a difficult and complex psychological process. . . . But the value of forgiveness is made explicit in the Christian Gospel, where Jesus actually forgives his murderers as he is on the cross. . . . And when speaking of prayer, which for Jesus was the key to communion with the Divine, he made it very plain: "Whenever you stand praying, forgive if you have anything against anyone, so that your Father who is also in heaven will forgive you your offences [Mark 11:25]". Clearly, Divine energy will not flow into you if you are unwilling to forgive—and move on with your life.

My abbreviated paraphrase of Stettbacher's four step method is:

Step 1: Describe your perception of the situation at hand where you are experiencing a problem.

Step 2: Describe the feelings and sensations associated with this problem situation.

Step 3: Try to unearth the reasons behind the feelings and sensations associated with the problem. Keep asking yourself the "why" behind each reason uncovered until you get to the root of the problem, if possible. It may be helpful to independently trace the root of each individual feeling or sensation.

Step 4: Now that you better understand the "whys" behind the problem, decide what you need to do about it. If you traced the root of each individual feeling or sensation, it may be most useful to define actions appropriate to each root traced.

If part of the "whys" behind the problem involves abuse by others, you will need to free yourself from your entanglement with them as part of what you need to do to be healed. That involves forgiveness.

The forgiveness process that worked for me is as follows:

1. Describe what they did to you: the abuse.
2. Describe your reaction to it:
    a. how you *felt* about the abuse and how it *affected you when it was happening*.
    b. how you *feel* about the abuse and how it *still affects you today*.
3. Describe your understanding of your abusers, then forgive them for being the kind of people who could abuse you. (Note: you are *not* forgiving them for the abuse itself—that's between them and God.)
4. Release them from *your* judgment, then release them to *God's* judgment and, if appropriate, the judicial system.
5. Claim your freedom from your abusers and feel the emotional release within yourself.

This begins your rehabilitation, or repentance, as you turn from judging them and claim your healing.

EXAMPLE ONE
OF MY VERSION OF STETTBACHER'S FOUR STEP METHOD :

Step 1: My perception of the situation where I was experiencing a problem.

- I woke up at 3:00 a.m. on the night of August 13, 1998, and was unable to go back to sleep.

Step 2: My associated feelings and sensations.

- My body feels tense; I'm not relaxed enough to sleep.
- I'm worried about my wife's health and our son's job interviews.

Step 3: The reasons behind the feelings and sensations associated with my problem.

a. I believe I'm responsible for situations that I worry about and have to fix them.

b. . . . because I have to be in control of everything if it's going to turn out right.

c. . . . because I can't trust anyone to do it right—not even God. I have to do it myself; I'm "Captain Rescue."

d. . . . because in my family of origin I tried to control my parents and prevent them from fighting by distracting them.

e. . . . because my parents' fighting terrified me.

f. . . . because when they fought I was afraid that my "safe" home would come to an end and I'd be abandoned.

Step 4: What I need to do about it.

a. Accept that I can't control either my wife or my son.

b. Turn them over to God: let go and let God.

c. Relax and go to sleep; forgive my parents in the morning.

Forgiveness letter to my parents

August 14, 1998
Dear Mom and Dad,

1. The abuse

For years I've held it against you that you did not provide me with a home where I felt safe and secure. Your dysfunctional relationship resulted in bitter verbal fights between you and what felt like conditional love for me. I only felt loved if I was a good boy and not when I messed up.

2a. Feelings and original effect of abuse

My feelings as a child were suppressed, since my anger, fear, and sadness were either shamed or punished.

2b. Current effect of abuse

As an adult, I'm out of touch with my emotions—I isolate from myself and others and am afraid of intimacy. I'm also usually emotionally unavailable, and abusive when angry. When I return to that time in my mind, I'm really angry, in fact, furious! I've led a sub-optimal existence for almost sixty years because of my upbringing by you two!

3. Understanding and forgiveness

I believe you could only show conditional love because that's what you received from your parents. I also believe you didn't love yourselves unconditionally, so you couldn't love me that way either. As well, I believe you felt threatened by my expressions of feelings. I believe you did the best could as parents, but you didn't give me what I needed as a child and so I've suffered much because of it. Nevertheless, I forgive you for being who you were and I repent of having judged you all these years. I accept your limitations.

4. Release from my to God's judgment

I release you from my judgment and turn you over to God.

5. Claim freedom and feel release

I claim my freedom from the bitter memories I had of you and our relationship. I feel the emotional release and am free to move on.

EXAMPLE TWO
OF MY VERSION OF STETTBACHER'S FOUR STEP METHOD

Step 1: My perception of the situation where I was experiencing a problem.

May 2, 2006 (This is a collection of what I see as related incidents.)

- I've had a number of dreams recently with a common theme: I screw up. I fear screwing up when I start something new.
- I'm sometimes uncomfortable in social situations involving people I'm not close to—e.g., other tenants in the apartment building where I live, meetings at church, out walking on the street. My common concern is that I might screw up by saying or doing the "wrong" thing.
- I'm unhappy with the relationship I have with each of my four children: I don't feel I've overcome my past screw-ups with them.
- I often wonder if I'm boring to others. Do I screw up by saying things that others don't find interesting?

Step 2: My associated feelings and sensations.

a. **Fear of screwing up**: saying or doing something wrong.

b. **General social anxiety**: feeling uneasy in social situations with no specific concern or fear.

c. **Loneliness**.

d. **General state of mind**: most of the time whereas I used to be unhappy, now I'm really happy!

Step 3: The reasons behind the feelings and sensations associated with my problem.

a. **I've been afraid of screwing up all my life**. For instance:

   i. I screwed up as a five-year-old by taking all the nails out of my wooden milk wagon. I destroyed the toy but thought I was doing well because I gave the "useful" nails to my Dad.

   ii. At sixteen, I screwed up taking down the upper porch at my parents' home. The porch joists ended up over the living room ceiling, which I damaged, and the hundred dollars my Dad saved by having me do the job he paid to have the ceiling repaired.

   iii. When I was nineteen, I screwed up telling my Dad about electricity. I told him there would be no current flowing through one light switch wire and he said there would be. I had just completed the section on electricity in university physics but my Dad had experience working for an electrical supply company. My Dad was right: I got a shock when I touched the wire.

   iv. I screwed up installing the microwave at my home. I didn't want to use the template provided for the installation "in case I ever needed it again," so I measured and my measurements were wrong. My son Trent finished the installation for me. That was a really tough period for me, and not long after that, in 1993, my wife and I separated.

v. I screwed up with my stock market investing in 2000–2003, losing over half of the value of my Retirement Savings Plan (RRSP). I did much better with my wife's RRSP, losing less than ten percent of hers.

But I've also done some things really well during my life. For instance:

i. As a child, I did well as an actor and in Arts and Letters festivals. With my newspaper route, I made enough money to buy a racing bike.

ii. I did okay working for a stock brokerage: they hired me for five summers.

iii. I did well as a computer programmer and systems analyst for six years. With the first company, I was put in a test unit which was disbanded when I left the company; with the second, they wanted to hire me back with a twenty-five percent raise after I got a PhD.

iv. I wrote an article on a unique approach to the then current view of pattern recognition in artificial intelligence applications, which was published in the refereed journal *Pattern Recognition* and received numerous requests for reprints, including several from behind the then "Iron Curtain."

v. I did okay as an MBA teacher for six years. I helped many students learn how to apply Behavioural Science theories and principles at work and I developed a useful course in "How to Solve Real-World Problems." More than twenty-five years later, former students I met still commented positively about those courses.

vi. I did well as an internal consultant with a large multinational corporation for fourteen years; they gave me many raises and monetary awards.

vii. I am really pleased with how I did as an external consultant with my own company for fourteen years; I satisfied many clients, exercised my creativity, and made a good living.

viii. I did okay in doing renovations on our homes: building a back deck, building back steps, shingling a sunroom roof, building a front walk and back patio, and repairing parging.

ix. I did a good job designing and having an R2000 vacation home built at our cottage property. I learned to competently operate and maintain a chainsaw as well as how to effectively maintain the cottage, and I built a "stepped walkway" down to the beach.

x. In handling legal issues: I won against a life insurance company and a paving contractor in Small Claims Court; I got my cottage neighbour to agree on my version of the boundary between our properties and to pay to repair the damage he'd done to my property; I won a more than $10,000 formal legal battle from the cottage builder regarding a water problem at the cottage; and I won a hydro line dispute there with Ontario Hydro that got them to move hydro poles and the easement to the property line, which would likely have cost over $50,000.

xi. I did a good job at Cedarview Community Church: I edited the church newspaper, started a viable Men's Group which I believe still continues today, and successfully developed a course on the Fundamentals of the Christian Faith.

xii. I am very pleased with how well I've done in developing an effective rational approach to forecasting recessions and to stock selection; this was my recovery from the stock market screw-up of 2000—2003.

In summary,

- **I've screwed up when I didn't take the time to carefully think through or prepare for what I needed to do;** I do well when I develop sufficient expertise in what I'm going to do.

b. **I've often been really anxious regarding social situations** because I was often mystified about the things that happened to me in social situations.

   i. I never understood *why* my parents had verbal fights. I got very good at predicting that they were *going to* verbally abuse each other but I never understood *why* (added October 26, 2007).

   ii. The father of a playmate, a big policeman, kicked me as I was sitting on the front steps of my childhood apartment home the day after the playmate and I had played together at my home. We were both about five years old and had had a good time playing together—I couldn't see *any* reason for it.

   iii. My friends would occasionally and all of a sudden be "bad friends" with me for no apparent reason.

   iv. I sometimes got bullied for no apparent reason.

   v. I never understood why some girls liked me and some didn't. However, I also never really knew why I was attracted to some girls and not others.

   vi. Sometimes, for reasons I didn't understand, people seemed to avoid or refrain from speaking to me. For instance, the President of the large multinational corporation where I was working didn't speak to me once when he and I were together in the elevator. I later learned he'd just found out two of his businesses had been unexpectedly sold out from under him by the parent corporation and he was preoccupied with that event. His indifference toward me had nothing to do with me.

vii. Sometimes I get the impression people don't like me or are annoyed with me for no apparent reason.

- I'm generally comfortable in situations with people I know or with family and friends.
    i. I do really well as a grandfather: I love and enjoy my grandchildren and they reciprocate.
- I feel less safe when I don't understand the "whys" behind what people say or do. In these instances the situations seem "out of control."
- People feel, think, and do things for their own reasons—just as I do! They don't have to understand my reasons to feel safe and neither do I have to understand their reasons to feel safe.
- I accept my grandchildren just as they are, but in social situations where I'm not comfortable, I don't accept others just as they are. I want to control the situation and have them act like I want them to, but I can't control others!
- **I don't accept that what others do is 100% about them and 0% about me and that what I do is 100% about me and 0% about others, even if I'm people-pleasing!**

c. I have been lonely—not intimate—almost all of my life.

i. It was not okay for me to feel my feelings of anger, fear, and sadness growing up as a child in my home, so I was isolated from myself. Today, I have a much better relationship with myself but it still usually takes me quite a while to become fully aware of my feelings.

ii. I was not intimate with my friends growing up—we were merely "doing" buddies.

iii. As an adult, I've had limited experiences of intimacy:

- In 1990, I had a week-long T-group experience where I began sensing and acting upon many feelings for the first time. Later in the 90s, I took a course on "getting in touch with feelings."
- In 1993, I started attending Adult Children of Alcoholics meetings and, soon after, Al-Anon meetings. These have been my great and ongoing encounter with feelings and intimacy.
- I have a few friends that I feel comfortable to share intimately with; I don't feel that way with other acquaintances.

iv. I was lonely with both my wives, but I couldn't have handled real intimacy with them if it had been offered.

- **I was not able to handle ongoing intimacy.** Routine intimacy was too different from my parents' home situation, so it was too threatening for me.
- **I was too out of touch with my own feelings.**
- **To give in to intimacy was to lose control and become too vulnerable.**

d. I have been unhappy most of my life.

i. I was unhappy in my home because I never knew if I'd be successful in keeping my parents from fighting. I was hyper-vigilant in watching them—so busy monitoring them I had no time to worry about my own feelings. The key was to maintain safety through control and the best feeling possible was "neutral." Feeling my own feelings would have distracted me from trying to control my parents.

ii. I always believed that I had to make others happy before it was safe for me to be happy; if I wasn't controlling the situation, it wasn't safe. This was true from grade school through my two marriages.

iii. As an adult, I believed it was okay to have "fun" only after all the jobs were done. My dad was the same way. Since all the jobs were almost never all done, there was very little time for fun; I have made far too little time for fun during most of my adult life. God spoke to me about leading a balanced life through my son Trent in 1988, but it took me nearly twenty years to be healed enough to act on that message!

Now, I'm happy most of the time.

i. Today, I lead a mostly balanced life: I build different non-work social or physical activities into most days, but I'm still working on improving the variety of activities in my life.

ii. In the social or volunteer activities I'm involved in, I make it a point to speak my mind; I deliberately do not people-please, which helps me really enjoy those activities. Sometimes others upset themselves by how they react to what I say!

- People-pleasing has been my biggest joy-robber.
- **Trying to control situations is my main reason for people-pleasing.**

Step 4: What I need to do about it.

a. Chronic fear of screwing-up.

Accept that I can't be good at everything. I do best when I carefully study something beforehand and when I develop sufficient expertise in the area.

b. General anxiety in social situations.

Accept that I can't control anyone else. This includes whether they like me or find me interesting or boring. In fact, I no longer want to try to control others, because trying to do that only makes me miserable. I have enough of a challenge running my own life. Also, I recognize that I resent others who I believe are trying to control me!

c. Chronic loneliness.

Accept that it takes time to develop close relationships. Continue to work on relationships and broaden my circle of friends.

Accept my children on their own terms, just as I do my grandchildren.

d. Chronic unhappiness.

Continue to lead a balanced life.

Develop a greater repertoire of activities.

EXAMPLE THREE
OF MY VERSION OF STETTBACHER'S 4 STEP METHOD.

Step 1: My perception of the situation where I was experiencing a problem.

As an adult, I have difficulty having fun on my own. When I'm with other adults or my grandkids I can do it, but when I'm by myself, I don't. To have fun seems like such a waste of time when there's so much to do and I worry that it won't all get done!

Step 2: My associated feelings and sensations.

I'm mildly disappointed and frustrated.

Step 3: The reasons behind the feelings and sensations associated with my problem.

a. I guess I don't strongly miss what I've never had as an adult.

b. . . . because there's always something else to do, so I'm not bored. Just to do something for the enjoyment of it seems a waste of time.

c. . . . because I'm uncomfortable if I have "nothing to do" or am doing "nothing." When my father stopped doing challenging work, he became senile.

d. . . . because I have difficulty being "fully present" for myself. Even when I'm eating, I distract myself by reading or watching TV. I don't want to take the time to really enjoy my food, but instead rush eating because taking the time to enjoy it seems like a waste of time. My father also wolfed down his food without tasting it. I jam up my daily schedule with jobs to do, leaving little time to relax and just "smell the roses." I'm letting life "pass me by" and losing the enjoyment of my "present moments."

e. . . . because I learned to be hyper-vigilant as a child, trying to pick up any signal that a "parental fight" was imminent. You can't be fully present for yourself if your focus is on others! So I've learned not to pay attention to my internal signals and can easily ignore them.

f. . . . because I was severely traumatized by the emotional turmoil in my parental home as a child. "Presence" would have meant feeling my terror, which I couldn't have dealt with as a child. So I learned, for survival reasons, to always focus on "outside me" and never on "inside me." I must learn and come to accept that "inside me" is now a safe place to be.

Step 4: What I need to do about it.

a. Start "being fully present" and "doing fun things," then do them on a regular basis and live with the initial discomfort.

b. Change my perspective to seeing "living life to the full" as normal and not "a waste of time." I found that my 2007 Florida vacation helped me to begin breaking the old mould and to start creating a new one, but I still have a long road to travel! I need to make specific concrete plans and then hold myself accountable for making them happen if I'm really going to do it. I must not accept my doing "more important stuff" like work as a valid excuse. For instance, I need to not work up until bedtime; instead, I need to relax before bedtime.

Tolle, in *The Power of Now*, says,

> Through allowing the "isness" of all things [fully accepting the reality of what is just as it is, without evaluation], a deeper dimension underneath the play of opposites reveals itself to you as an abiding presence, an unchanging deep stillness, an uncaused joy beyond good and bad. This is the joy of Being, the peace of God (183).

God then spoke to me about the healing I needed.

Friday April 4, 2008 A.M.

My Question: What would you say to me today, Lord?

The "Still Small Voice" Answer: "Thank you, My son, for the respect shown. Enjoy your busy and life-changing day, My beloved son. You will enjoy this day, but find it difficult—and even frightening. Enjoy it as best you are able, My beloved son. Enjoy your day!"

It was difficult for me to decide to start to attempt being fully present for myself, but I did it. It was fearful—and exciting—to contemplate leaving behind a lifetime of hyper-vigilance toward others and inattention to my own internal state and imagine focussing ongoing attention on what's going on inside of me!

I scheduled my start date as April 8, 2008, when I decided to try to eat breakfast without reading or watching TV. I wanted to focus solely on tasting and enjoying my food *and nothing else*! To do that, I knew I'd need to leave myself enough time to eat slowly and with enjoyment, for if I felt rushed, I wouldn't taste my food! I decided that once I had mastered that first, I would go on to my other meals and then to other solitary activities in my life.

I actually started with lunch on April 5, 2008. Since then, I take the time to taste at least one meal a day—usually more. I was surprised how tasty my food actually was. In order to really focus on tasting my food, I kept my eyes closed the whole time I was chewing. After a couple of weeks, I started tasting with my eyes open. I was frequently distracted by thoughts running through my mind but kept bringing my attention back to the food. And not long after I began working on enjoying eating, before going to bed I started listening to peaceful music, doing some reading, or watching some pleasant TV program to aid my pre-sleep relaxation. As a result, I've started, typically, to have a longer, better sleep at night.

I do a daily morning and night "spot inventory" of my internal state. On May 21, 2008, in the morning, I paid attention to the observation that, first thing in the morning and last thing at night, I'm tense. This was not a new thing—it's been that way all the many years I've been taking these spot inventories. As I was reflecting on this, God spoke to me in His "still small voice" saying, "*And yes, My son, you are tense because the remnants of your hyper-vigilance are still active. I love you, My beloved son. Take the chance and show the love for yourself to become free of this, My beloved son. And you shall then truly be joyful. Do this and live fully, My beloved son. Enjoy all your days!"*

I believe what I need to do is to work at being fully present much/most/all of the time. To achieve this, I will use the different approaches to being fully present identified by Tolle, as described in Appendix 1.

After taking a couple days to develop and mull over a preliminary plan, I did an initial implementation on my walk on the afternoon of May 29, 2008. During that walk, I attempted *all* of Tolle's "being fully present" exercises in the order listed and I was pleased with how peaceful I felt after I was done. But I was still having difficulty going back to sleep after waking up at night because I would worry or think with excitement about something that I was going to be doing the next day.

Then, on Monday morning July 14, 2008, God spoke to me in His "still small voice" saying, "*My son, you do well to be displeased in yourself because you do not turn your worries over to Me. Do this and live more fully.*" Since then, I turn my worries and excitement over to God, so going back to sleep after waking at night has become much easier.

In finishing this book, I had a "workaholic relapse" and God spoke to me on the evening of September 4, 2008, saying "*My son, you work too hard—too much. When you do that, you are not loving yourself. To write about it and not practice it is foolish and unloving. Stop this insanity now! Enjoy a balanced life. You do not bless me by abusing yourself.*"

I *will* love myself no matter what! This is the ongoing challenge of the rest of my life!

EXAMPLE FOUR

OF MY VERSION OF STETTBACHER'S 4 STEP METHOD.

On November 1, 2008, I determined to directly address my workaholism.

Step 1: My perception of the situation where I was experiencing a problem.

I almost always delay taking the time to fully enjoy the moment (love myself) because I almost always have something more important to do, which is almost always *work*. I can take the time to *enjoy myself later; work is more important now*!

Step 2: My associated feelings and sensations.

I'm somewhat disappointed but I'm becoming increasingly frustrated with myself because "tomorrow almost never seems to come" and I'm almost 70!

In late October, I had the insight that as long as I continue to behave in an unloving (insane) manner, I will not be completely healed. There is *never* a good excuse to do the unloving thing, to behave in an unloving manner. There is *no* excuse!

As I continued to mull this insight over in my mind, God spoke to me on the morning of October 27: "*Do not be disappointed, My son. As you are realizing, you must take the time to truly focus on the areas where you are not loving yourself and deal with them before you are truly healed.*"

Step 3: The reasons behind the feelings and sensations associated with my problem.

a. When I was employed, I justified delaying enjoying myself "because of my job." When I was self-employed, I justified delaying enjoying myself "because of my customers." Now that I'm retired, I justify delaying enjoying myself "because of my project"—for instance, this book. The truth is that it's not jobs, customers, or projects, but *me, as it's always been*!

b. Because it's not a "big deal" for me to put off living life to the full, since that's what I've *always* done, ever since childhood.

c. Because as a child, my focus was on preventing my parents from fighting, and not on my own feelings of fear and sadness.

d. Because focussing on my feelings might have led to my not doing my job, which was to keep my world safe by preventing my parents from fighting.

e. Because if I don't complete my job, my world will be unsafe, so jobs are more important than me! Jobs give me my self-worth–I have no inherent self-worth!

f. Because I don't fully accept that I'm a *child of God*, which gives me *inherent* self-worth!

Step 4: What I need to do about it.

1. *Never* make anything more important than loving myself.
2. *Always* take the time to be fully present (aware of what's going on inside of me) before beginning *every* activity.
3. *Periodically* during the activity, take a reading of my internal state.

AFTERWORD

Now having written this book, I feel a kinship with two people from the past. One is Mother Theresa, and the other Albert Einstein. Let me explain.

Albert Einstein was a Swiss Patent Clerk when he proposed the Theory of Relativity, not an eminent Professor of Physics. I am neither a Professor of Theology nor a theologian, but I have been a scholar, and I am a long-time student of the Bible, which I have read through completely, on average, once a year for the past 30 years.

When Mother Theresa was interviewed for the TV Program "60 Minutes" not long after having been awarded the 1979 Nobel Prize for Peace, one of the CBS staffers commented on his encounter with her. He said that the famous people who had been interviewed for the program tended to be one way in front of the camera and another way—less humble or gracious—behind the scenes. But Mother Theresa was not one of those. When this staffer tried to flatter her and take the focus away from God, she cut him off with the statement, "I'm just a little pencil in God's Hand." That "Little Pencil" had a wonderful ministry of loving care to the forgotten ones dying on the streets of Calcutta.

I believe that God inspired my understanding of most, if not all, of the topics covered in this book. And while He did not tell me to write the book, He also did not ask me to stop. My hope is that this "Pencil" was faithful to the inspiration received and will bless "seekers of solid food," provide comfort to those whom the church has confused or turned its back on, and help others discover that God is real.

Rob Bell, in *Velvet Elvis*, speaks of the need "to keep reforming . . . I mean theology, the beliefs about God, Jesus, the Bible, salvation, the future. We must keep reforming the way the Christian faith is defined, lived, and explained" (12). I believe the proposals in this book represent that kind of meaningful reform.

One final comment: The focus of this book has been on important truths about God that can be inferred from the Bible. In the process of defining those truths, some of my statements may appear to some as having been made in an ungracious manner. My intent, however, was accuracy, not ungraciousness (Galatians 1:10).

Marvellously, the God I've written about is *always* gracious! Try God for yourself and experience that wonderful life-giving grace. As Psalm 34:8 says, "Taste and see that the Lord is good."

APPENDIX 1

Contents

Homosexuals

God loves homosexuals just as much as heterosexuals—no more and no less (John 3:16–17). However, homosexual sex and heterosexual sex between unmarried couples are both sin. Leviticus 18:20 states that adultery is a sin: "Do not have sexual relations with your neighbour's [someone else's] wife and defile yourself with her"; Leviticus 18:22 states that sodomy is a sin: "Do not lie with a man as one lies with a woman; that is detestable"; Numbers 25:1-8 describes an unmarried man and woman receiving punishment for fornicating and Romans 1:26 speaks against female homosexual sex: "Even . . . women exchanged natural relations for unnatural ones," then compares those "unnatural relations" to sodomy in verse 27.

However, I believe the scriptural basis for the strongest condemnation of homosexuality today comes from the interpretation attached to the significance of the destruction of Sodom (from which "sodomy" derives its name) and Gomorrah (Genesis 18:20–19:25). "Then the Lord said, 'The outcry against Sodom and Gomorrah is so great and their sin so grievous that I will go down and see if what they have done is as bad as the outcry that has reached me. If not, I will know'" (18:20–21). An omniscient and omnipresent God did not have to go down there to find out if their citizens were engaging in homosexual sex—He already knew they had a long history of "homosexual sex." So what is the "badness" that God was looking for?

The unfolding of the incident with Lot and his two male figure angelic guests lets us see what that "badness" was: "They [the men of Sodom] called to Lot, 'Where are the men who came to you tonight? Bring them out to us so we can have sex with them'" (19:5). In other words, they *intended to rape* Lot's guests, which represents a *lack of love* and *homosexual lust* for those guests. At this point, the visitors tell Lot, "Get . . . out of here, because we are going to destroy this place" (19:12–13), which they do (19:24–25).

An incident of *rape* representing a similar *lack of love* as well as both homosexual and *heterosexual lust* led to the destruction of the Tribe of Benjamin (Judges 19:1–20:48). Taking the Sodom and Gomorrah narrative out of the context of the rest of the Bible leads to the *isegetical* interpretation that the sin punished was *homosexuality*, rather than the sins of *lack of love* and *lust*!

Evangelical churches often have signs saying "Sinners welcome," so they should welcome fornicating heterosexuals, homosexuals, those who cheat on their taxes and on their spouses and all other sinners. The only sinners who should be *excluded* are those who *promote a sinful lifestyle within the church*! To make homosexual sex out to be a greater sin than the sins common among evangelicals is the sin of *pride*, as demonstrated in the parable of the Pharisee and the Tax Collector (Luke 18:9–14)!

Typical Holy Spirit Counsel Example

Friday October 26, 2007 A.M.

My Question: What would you say to me today, Lord?

The "Still Small Voice" Answer: "My son, you have slept well enough for now [about six and one half hours; I napped in the afternoon]. Enjoy a less busy day, My beloved son, but be prepared for possible *surprises* this day, My beloved son."

The *surprise* was a request, less than an hour after God had spoken to me, to take two of my granddaughters, both age seven, on an outing to a local farm that had already been scheduled for the *next* day (Saturday). So that's what I did: I changed my plans and took my two granddaughters out instead, and we all had a good time.

Explanation: Friday October 26, 2007, turned out to be a Professional Activities day for teachers and thus, a day off from school for these two granddaughters. Also the weather forecast for Saturday was for rain, so Friday seemed the better/safer choice. There was actually rain for much of Saturday, which would have made our visit to the farm on that day much less enjoyable.

A Recovery Fairy Tale

Once upon a time, in the Kingdom of Challabund, a baby boy was born to a peasant couple living in a humble cottage. They loved God, themselves, each other, and other people, and so baby Kwijert, for that's what they called him, grew up receiving lots of love from his parents.

However, with the neighbourhood boys it was a different story. As Kwijert grew, the local peasant boys made fun of him because he was different than they were. He was too gentle— not boisterous and noisy, not cruel to animals, and he did not bully the smaller and weaker boys like they did. His parents spoke to some of the other peasant couples about the situation, but nothing changed.

When Kwijert became a young man, his parents understood that he wanted to leave home and seek his fortune. As he was leaving, his mother gave him a big loaf of bread, a slab of cheese, and a large flask of wine, and his father gave him a small purse filled with gold coins. Kwijert put everything in his knapsack, bid a fond farewell to his parents and went on his way.

Kwijert travelled through the neighbouring kingdoms, spending some time in each. In all of the kingdoms, he hired out as a peasant labourer, working with the young men of the kingdom. The masters always appreciated him, for he was a hard worker as well as honest and clever, but with his fellow labourers it was always the same old story. Kwijert found these young men similar to those in Challabund. So, when he'd had enough of their company and—if the truth be known—the young men had had enough of his, Kwijert took his leave of the kingdom and left for a new one, usually much to the chagrin of the master.

At long last, in the wilderness along the road to yet another kingdom, he became discouraged and said out loud to no one in particular, for the closest person was miles away, "Is there no kingdom on earth where the young men are like me? Men who are gentle and caring and not roustabouts? Men who want to be counsellors and healers and not knights and fighters?"

At that very moment, an angel appeared to him and said, "Ho Kwijert, my good fellow—don't lose heart. Continue your travels, and when you reach the Kingdom of Integreal, which is only twelve kingdoms further, you will receive your wish. To get there, though, you must take the *chemin de retablissement* rather than the *rue ordinaire*."

Much encouraged, Kwijert travelled on, taking the *chemin de retablissement*.

The next nine kingdoms were mostly like the previous ones, although not as bad, for he would occasionally find men to his liking. By the fifth kingdom, Kwijert had started to acknowledge his own shortcomings, and by the ninth he was getting along better with his co-workers. But when he reached the tenth, he began to really be encouraged. There the young men were understanding and accepting of each other, and in the eleventh, they were also gentle and caring. Finally, when Kwijert reached the twelfth, the Kingdom of Integreal, he knew he'd found his dream kingdom. The brave people there were gentle and caring, and they were renowned for their counsellors and healers.

Overjoyed, Kwijert soon apprenticed himself to a counsellor-healer. After some years, he established his own practice and was soon renowned throughout the land. During that time, he met and married Wemad, who was also a counsellor-healer, and they raised a loving family and lived happily ever after. During his lifetime, he never again returned to Challabund, his parents' kingdom.

On his deathbed, the angel who had spoken to him many years earlier came to him again and said, "You have done well with your life. But what you do not realize is that the people in the Kingdoms of Challabund and Integreal and in all the other kingdoms are very similar. It was not the other people that changed, it was *you*! You finally accepted yourself for *who you are* and the other young men for *who they are*. But it took you many years to get to that point."

And so the sadness from his memories of the boys and young men of his past that Kwijert had kept inside for all those years began to leave him, because on his deathbed he realized that his earlier judgments had been hasty. Kwijert reflected back on his past in Challabund, as well as all the other kingdoms he had experienced, and recalled that not all the boys and men he had interacted with were bullies. And even in Integreal, some of the people he'd encountered were bullies. As a flood of memories engulfed him, he first recalled Artful, a decent boy from Challabund; then he remembered men from the other kingdoms he had visited who were also decent folk. Finally, the male clients from his counselling practice in Integreal who had been bullies came to mind—men he'd gotten to know intimately—and he remembered the human frailties he'd learned of; frailties that had been the result of their coping with a difficult childhood. And a serene peace swept over him.

Then he died content in the sleep of peace, with a smile on his face.

Approaches to Presence

The following are adaptations and enhancements from material in Tolle's *The Power of Now*. I've listed them in the order I'll likely find easiest to most difficult. For exercises 2–4, I will likely find it easier if I CLOSE MY EYES.

1. Be totally present in what I'm already doing.
    a. What are the things that I SEE—their colours, shapes, etc.?
    b. What are the things that I HEAR—tones, volume, pleasantness, nature/man-made, etc.?
    c. What are the things that I SMELL—sharpness, strength, pleasantness, specific odours that I recognize, etc.?
    d. What are the TASTES in my mouth—sweet/sour/salty/bitter, my breath, etc.?
    e. What are the TOUCHING sensations I am aware of—the clothes on my skin, the socks or shoes on my feet, the contact of my hands? What are the pressures, aches/pains, pleasantnesses, etc. that I notice?
2. Focus on my body.
    a. Start with my extremities (hands/arms and feet/legs), then be aware of my back/chest, then my head, and finally, my gut (stomach/intestines/etc.).
3. Focus on my breathing.
    a. Feel each breath, the expansion/contraction of my chest/abdomen, etc.

4. Observe what is going on inside of me at this moment. The key is to just observe it and not be critical of what I find or try to change it—just observe it.

    a. What thoughts are flowing through my mind right now?

    b. What feelings am I aware of having right now: happy/sad, fear/anger, etc.?

    c. What else is going on inside of me right now: tension/excitement, discomfort/pleasurable sensations, etc.?

    d. What "pain bodies" am I aware of right now?

APPENDIX 2

POSITION PAPER

ON

DEALING EFFECTIVELY WITH

VIOLENT OFFENDERS

SO AS TO

REALLY MAKE CANADA SAFER

2007 - Ken Tunstall, PhD
Prison Volunteer

EXECUTIVE SUMMARY

The position paper summarizes the key profile data on violent offenders, and proposes improvements to the effectiveness of their treatment by Correctional Services Canada.

Who are the violent offenders? The profile of the typical Canadian violent offender is: a single male Caucasian from a dysfunctional family first arrested as a juvenile with a record of prior incarceration who is an unemployed substance abuser lacking high school education and having an unstable job history.

How did they become violent offenders? Their family background typically includes violence, where they learn to 'act out' violently.

What is their recidivism rate? The probability of repeat incarceration during their lifetime exceeds 80%.

How can they be rehabilitated? Correctional Services Canada currently has effective programs for Violence Prevention, Substance Abuse Treatment, Education and Employment. However, these programs are currently not made available to all violent offenders. They need to be made available to all violent offenders. Also, the employment skills programs need to be expanded.

What else needs to be done with violent offenders? Once a violent offender commits their second violent offense, they should remain incarcerated until assessed as rehabilitated. To release a violent offender who still has tendencies to violence and lacks the education & job skills to earn a decent living while still having a substance abuse problem is a recipe that ensures failure—recidivism! This is unfair both to the violent offender and the community into which he is released.

Ordinary Canadians are supportive of this position, based on numerous informal discussions.

TABLE OF CONTENTS

A. WHO ARE THE VIOLENT OFFENDERS?

The following composite portrait of the violent Canadian offender emerges from the papers by Bonta & Motiuk, Bonta & Yessine, Matarazzo, and Motiuk, Boe & Cousineau:

1. Having prior incarceration: 86- 88.5%,
2. First arrested as a juvenile: 75%,
3. Being a Caucasian male: 84.4%,
4. Lacking a High School Diploma: 78%,
5. Unemployed: 63.3-78.1%
6. Having an unstable job history: 73%,
7. Drug or alcohol abuser: 80%,
8. Single: 54.7-66.6%,
9. Having some general personality disorder: 71.1%,
10. Claiming dysfunctional family background: 53%.

A related pattern emerges from a UK study of 411 male career criminals, as described in the Correctional Services Canada paper on the lifespan of criminal behaviour in the section "What do we know?":

1. Longer criminal careers for those first convicted at age 16 or earlier,
2. Longer criminal careers for heavy drinkers frequently unemployed during teen-age years who rarely spent leisure time with a father,
3. Progressively increasing recidivism probabilities: after one offence (68%), after 2 offences (71.2%), after 3 or more offences (80-90%),
4. About 1/3 of total offences were violent.

The US Bureau of Justice Statistics report of jailed inmates concludes:

1. 40% had a violent offence in their history,
2. 53% were on probation, parole or pretrial release at the time of arrest,

3. 75% of convicted jail inmates were alcohol or drug-involved at the time of their current offence,
4. 31% of jail inmates had grown up with a parent or guardian who abused alcohol or drugs, and 46% had a family member who had been incarcerated.

An abstract of the results of the study by Putkonen *et al* states that among violent Finnish female offenders, "81% were diagnosed with a personality disorder."

As the above papers illustrate, the characteristics of violent offenders cut across lines of national and sexual identity.

A. REFERENCES

1. Bonta, J. & Motiuk, L. L. High-risk violent offenders in Canada. *American Psychological Association*, 1996 (August), presentation paper.
2. Bonta, J. & Yessine, A.K. The national flagging system. *Public Safety and Emergency*, 2005, PS33-1/2005-3.
3. Bureau of Justice Statistics *Recidivism of prisoners released in 1994*, 2002(06), NCJ 19 3427.
4. Correctional Services of Canada The life span of criminal behaviour. *Forum Recidivism*, 1993, *V*(3).
5. Matarazzo, A. Court referrals for a group of youth and young adults. *Statistics Canada*, 2006, 11-008-XWE.
6. Motiuk, L., Boe, R. & Cousineau, C. The safe return of offenders to the community-2004. *Correctional Operations and Program Research Board*, 2004(April).
7. Putkonen, H., Komulainen, E. J., Virkkunen, M., Eronen, M. & Lonnqvist, J. Risk of repeat offending among violent female offenders with psychotic and personality disorders. *American Journal of Psychiatry*, 2003, *160:947-51*.

B. HOW DID THEY GET TO BE VIOLENT OFFENDERS?

In their summary and conclusions based on Canadian data, Alksnis & Taylor state "Research conducted with children indicates that children who are both witnesses and victims of abuse have more severe aggressive behavioural outcomes than do those who are solely victims, who in turn have more difficulties than those who have witnessed violence but have never been victimized. Investigations conducted with adolescents and adults in the general population suggest that both witnessing and experiencing family violence in childhood are associated with violence in the adult family. Research with offenders indicates a very high proportion of this population have a history of witnessing violence or being directly victimized. . . . The correspondence between criminal and family abuser profiles reinforces the importance of making treatment programs available to offenders [pp.1-2]."

The article by Motiuk, Boe & Cousineau cited in part A states on page 11 that 53% of federal inmates claim to have had dysfunctional parents. In Cermak's book, he states that "a person is more likely to develop symptoms of PTSD [post-traumatic stress disorder] if the trauma is experienced while the person is living in a closed social system [e.g., a family]. . . . Alcoholic families create many of the same stresses for children as those that exist in combat. . . . [The] four major symptoms of post-traumatic stress disorder [are: *reexperiencing of the trauma, psychic numbing, hypervigilance,* and *survivor guilt [p.77].* Psychic numbing [includes] A sense of depersonalization. . . . Not fitting into one's surroundings. . . . A feeling of emotional anesthesia. . . . Constriction of emotions, especially in situations demanding intimacy, tenderness, or sexuality. . . . The symptoms of PTSD continue to exist until an active process of healing occurs [pp. 86–7]." Jean Vanier makes the point that "If we feel we have no worth, it is because we have been told, in one way or another, that this is so. We will then act accordingly; we will hurt others precisely because we know we have no worth and can only do worthless things [p.137]."

That criminals come from dysfunctional backgrounds and are ineffectively handled by the criminal justice system is no surprise to most Canadians. According to Stein's summary of opinion polls, "The majority of Canadians perceive social factors, such as poor parenting and broken homes, as the primary cause of crime [p.1]." and "Canadians do not have a lot of confidence in the criminal justice system, in particular the courts and corrections [p.3]."

It is unjust to further abuse the abused criminal rather than attempt to rehabilitate him. It is unjust both to the Canadian criminal (programmed through no fault of his own to emit violent behaviour) and to the Canadian public, re-subjected to his violent behaviour through his recidivism after release.

B. REFERENCES

1. Alksnis, C. & Taylor, J. A. The impact of experiencing and witnessing family violence during childhood. *Correctional Services of Canada*, 2003, FV04.
2. Cermak, T. L. *A time to heal.* New York: Avon Books, 1988.
3. Vanier, J. *Becoming human.* [Massey lecture] Toronto, Ananasi, 1998.
4. Stein, K. [Executive Summary] Public perception of crime and justice in Canada. *Department of Justice Canada*, 2001(November); updated 2005(October).

C. WHAT IS THE RECIDIVISM OF VIOLENT OFFENDERS?

Recidivism is an ambiguous term. It can be used to refer to parole violation, re-arrest, re-conviction, or re-incarceration, and the time period can be from 2 years to the offender's lifetime. Where possible, this paper uses the term to refer to re-incarceration.

The article by Motiuk, Boe, & Cousineau cited in part A states that "87% of new federal offenders have previously been in prison either as young offenders or in a provincial adult institution [p.3]." The paper by Nafekh & Motiuk states that the recidivism rate of federal offenders ranges from 6% (those judged to be a good risk not to reoffend) to 44% (those judged a poor risk not to reoffend). Their paper further states that recidivism is reduced by education (21.3% reduction with grade 10, 7.1% reduction with grade 8), employment training (27.8% reduction for completion of the prison industries program), substance abuse program (31.9% reduction in new convictions), cognitive skills training (20% reduction in new convictions), and anger management (86% reduction in violent recidivism).

The Correctional Services of Canada article on the UK study of 411 male career criminals cited in part A, in the section "What do we know" states that "The average duration of criminal careers dropped sharply from those first convicted between the ages of 14 and 16 (8.2 years) to those first convicted between 17 and 20 (2.7 years). ... Overall, more than three quarters (78.3%) of those convicted as juveniles were also convicted as adults. ... Research on criminal careers also focuses on recidivism probabilities, which are often very high. For example, of the 153 participants who committed one offence, more than two thirds (68%) went on to commit another offence by age 32. Of the 104 men who committed a second offence, almost three quarters (71.2%) went on to commit a third. From the third offence on, the probability of recidivism was almost always between 80% and 90% [p.3]." The same article looks at 3348 Canadian offenders (3267 male) in the section "Recidivists tend to be" and states that "Of the 3,267 [male] inmates, nearly half (44%) re-offended in the three year follow-up period [p.2]." Again, the same article looks at the US experience with Intensive Supervision Probation (ISP) Programs in the section "Does punishing smarter work?" and draws a number of conclusions "...high risk offenders in the ISP had recidivism rates 30% lower than those on regular probation [p.4]." "In both the ISP program and the regular supervision group, recidivism rates were 12% to 33% lower among offenders whose probation officer offered high-quality as opposed to low quality supervision [p.5]."

Bonta, Rugge, & Dauvergne state that "The median rate for re-arrest was 62.5%, for re-conviction 46.8%, and for re-incarceration 25.4% [p.2]." "In general, the longer the follow-up, the higher the recidivism [p.3]." "[The median violent crime re-offence rate, excluding first & second degree murder, was 62.6% p.11]."

In the highlights of their article, Hughes & Wilson indicate that the % of released US violent offenders who were re-arrested within 3 years in 1983 & 1994 is over 60%. Freeman, on page 18 gives the same figures & states that 12% were homeless at the time of arrest (p.19). In an abstract of his paper on US prisoners, Harer states "Within 3 years of their release...in 1987, 40.8% of these inmates had recidivated." In an abstract of their paper on US recidivism, Blumstein & Graddy state "The probability of re-arrest for an index [serious] crime is estimated as 85 to 90 percent for both whites and blacks."

The conclusion is clear: violent offenders are very likely to reoffend. The greater the number of prior offences and the longer the time since the last offence, the greater the likelihood. The Canadian data are consistent with Blumstein & Graddy's US data: over 80% probability of recidivism.

C. REFERENCES

1. Bonta, J., Rugge, T. & Dauvergne, M. The reconviction rate of federal offenders, 2003-02, *Public Works and Government Services Canada*, Cat. No. JS42-100/2002E-IN.

2. Blumstein, A. & Graddy, E. Prevalence and recidivism in index arrests. *Law & Society Review*, 1981-2, *16(2)*, 265-90.

3. Freeman, R. Can we close the revolving door? *Urban Institute Reentry Roundtable Discussion Paper*, 2005.

4. Hughes, T. & Wilson, D.J. Reentry trends in the United States. *Bureau of Justice Statistics*, 2003.

5. Nafekh, M. & Motiuk, L.L. The statistical information on recidivism-revised 1 (SIR-R1) scale. *Correctional Services of Canada Research Bureau*, 2002 (November) No. R-126.

D. HOW CAN VIOLENT OFFENDERS BE REHABILITATED?

According to Motiuk, Boe, & Cousineau (cited in part A) "Legally, the CSC [Correctional Services of Canada] operates under the 1992 Correction and Conditional Release Act. It states that the purpose of the federal corrections system is to contribute to the maintenance of a just, peaceful, and safe society by:

Carrying out the sentences imposed by the courts through the safe and humane custody and supervision of offenders, and

Assisting in the rehabilitation of offenders and their reintegration into the community as law-abiding citizens through the provision of programs in the penitentiaries and in the community [p.2]."

1. What doesn't work

The 2 papers by Gendreau & Goggin and their colleagues are based on an extensive review and data analysis of the existing multinational (mostly US) literature on the effects of incarceration and the threat of sanctions. The stated conclusion in the abstract of the Smith, Goggin & Gendreau paper is "The overall findings showed that harsher criminal justice sanctions had no deterrent effect on recidivism. On the contrary, punishment produced a slight (3%) increase in recidivism." The 2 papers also conclude that the threat of longer sentences had no impact on re-offence rate, and they both cite the estimate of $1,000,000 as the lifetime cost of incarcerating a career high risk offender.

Clearly, more punishment by imprisonment is a very expensive and ineffective way of dealing with the problem of recidivism. Imprisonment alone does not rehabilitate offenders! Karl Menninger, the noted American Psychiatrist, came to the same conclusion over 30 years ago, as described in his book "The crime of punishment".

A couple of prison volunteer anecdotes poignantly illustrate the same point:

a. 'Jane', the first born in her family, at the age of 2 was witnessing her drunken father punching her very pregnant mother in the stomach while saying 'It's probably just another girl'. Jane tried to stop him and for her efforts was thrown out of the second story of their dwelling into the snow which cushioned her fall. Frightened and angry, she came back in and again unsuccessfully tried to stop her father's violent behaviour. Fifteen years later, a pregnant & unwed Jane is being punched in the stomach by a female companion. The attack triggers Jane back to the incident when she was 2 and she violently assaults the companion for which she is incarcerated. It seems clear that if she is not healed/rehabilitated, Jane will again act out her childhood pain after release if similarly triggered.

b. 'Joe' assaulted a service station attendant during a robbery with an aluminum base ball bat for which he was sentenced to 5 years imprisonment. Joe told that as he was assaulting the attendant, he was seeing his mother. Joe was not healed/rehabilitated, and was re-incarcerated within 9 months of his release.

2. What does work

"In the last two decades, evidence has moved away from the 'nothing works' (Martinson, 1974) perspective to repeatedly demonstrating that even the highest risk offenders can benefit from effective treatment programs (Andrews & Bonta, 2003) [Cortoni, Nunes & Latendresse, p.1]."

In an interesting and valuable assessment of the California Correctional System, Petersillia says "The state's approach to corrections is enormously expensive—and enormously ineffective. Although California spent more than $7 billion on its correctional system in 2005-2006, it produced one of the highest recidivism rates in the nation. . . . California has the largest prison population of any state in the nation, with 168,000 inmates in 33 adult prisons. . . . California's prisons currently operate at nearly 200% of their intended capacity, making them dramatically overcrowded [p.1]." Petersillia makes a number of sensible improvement suggestions. "Each suggestion . . . is oriented toward creating the structural changes to facilitate the re-introduction of rehabilitation as a meaningful concept in California corrections. . . .

"Prioritize the delivery of programs that may actually help inmates address their profound and widespread problems with substance abuse, lack of education, and lack of job skills. . . .

"Employ parole supervision in a more selected and concentrated way, so that it targets the most likely re-offenders. . . .

"Develop program changes on the basis of *solid research* and *empirical evidence* suggesting the effectiveness of whatever modifications are implemented. Rigorously designed studies demonstrating the effectiveness of particular programs in reducing recidivism will increase public support for such programs, and, more importantly, improve the odds that the programs will improve public safety [p.4]."

a. Diagnosis of Risk

The Nafekh & Motiuk paper (cited in part C) describes an assessment tool, the SIR (Statistical Information on Recidivism) scale. It "combines 15 items in a scoring system that yields probability estimates of re-offending within three years of release. Each item is a measure of a demographic or criminal history characteristic. . . . [This scale] has proven to be a consistent and valid predictor of post-release outcome over time [p.11]." The 15 items in the SIR scale are 1. Current Offence 2. Age at Admission 3. Previous Incarceration 4. Revocation or Forfeiture [of parole or other release conditions] 5. Act of Escape 6. Security Classification [maximum security classification or not] 7. Age at First Adult Conviction 8. Previous Convictions for Assault 9. Marital Status at Most Recent Admission 10. Interval at Risk Since Last Offence [2 or more years in the community since last conviction] 11. Number of Dependents at Most Recent Admission 12. Current Total Aggregate Sentence 13. Previous

Convictions for Sex Offences 14. Previous Convictions for Break and Enter 15. Employment Status at Arrest [p.26]." The success rate with violent offenders, both non-aboriginal and aboriginal, ranges from 99% for those assessed as a very good risk to a rate for poor risk offenders of 88.7%(aboriginal males), 93.3%(non-aboriginal males), and 96.2%(females) [pp.41-2]." Clearly an impressive risk assessment tool.

b. Mitigating the Risk

i. Violence Prevention The paper by Cortoni, Nunes & Latendresse describes success with the Violence Prevention Program (VPP). They state 'The VPP is divided into 3 phases: intake screening, intervention [The 10 modules, presented in 94-2 hour sessions, are 1. Making Change, 2. Violence Awareness, 3. Anger Control, 4. Solving Problems, 5. Social Attitudes, 6. Positive Relationships, 7. Conflict Resolution, 8. Positive Lifestyles, 9. Self-Control, 10. Violence Prevention], and post-treatment assessment [pp.1-2]." In terms of VPP success, the incidence of violent recidivism was 8.5% [91.5% success rate] for those who completed the entire program (333 inmates), 24.5% for those inmates who did not complete the entire program (167 inmates), and 21.5% for those inmates who did not take the program at all (466 inmates) [p.25]. The authors conclude "The results from this study provide encouraging evidence that the VPP is an effective intervention in reducing recidivism for both Aboriginal and non-Aboriginal offenders, but only for those offenders who complete the full program[pp. 33-4]." Recall that the paper by Nafekh & Motiuk cited in part B found an 86% success rate with anger management alone.

ii. Substance Abuse Treatment Ettner *et al* state "Our best estimate is that, on average, substance abuse treatment costs $1.583 and is associated with a societal benefit of $11,487 [to the California taxpayer], representing a 7:1 ratio of benefits to costs (9:1 when arrest data are 'inflated' to proxy for actual crimes committed). This ratio is based on weighted average treatment costs, which reflect expected costs of treatment, 9 months follow-up of clients in all modalities with follow-up survey data, so that as many sources of benefits as possible could be included in the analysis; and benefit measures that demonstrate significant change, so that the estimates are robust to rare events. Sixty-five percent of the total benefit was attributable to reduction in crime costs, including incarceration. Twenty-nine percent was because of increased employment earnings, with the remaining 6 percent because of reduced medical and behavioral health costs[pp. 14-5]." In their executive summary, Marsteller, Rolka & Falek state '"The offenders who do not attend the program recidivate at twice the rate of those who attend [the Georgia DUI Alcohol/Drug Risk Prevention Program]." The Motiuk, Boe & Cousineau paper (cited in part A) reviews several Canadian substance abuse programs and finds re-conviction rates reduced by 28.6-50% for those completing the program.

iii. <u>Anti-Social Attitude Treatment</u> The Correctional Services of Canada study concluded that the Counter-Point Program reduces anti-social attitudes and recidivism as compared to those who did not complete the program or a matched comparison group. "Overall decreases in tendencies to blame other factors and an increase in accepting personal responsibility for crime were related to reduction in criminal behaviour. . . . [Completion] of the Counter-Point Program was associated with a 30% reduction in the risk of having . . . committed a new offence following release[pp.59-60]."

iv. <u>Education & Employment Programs</u> In the executive summary of their research report, Porporino & Robinson state " [In a large initial study of 1736 offenders, only]

30.1% of the ABE [Adult Basic Education] completers had readmission during the follow-up period compared to 35.5% of those who were released before completing and 41.6% of the offenders who had withdrawn from ABE. . . . [T]hose offenders who possess 'high risk' characteristics appeared to benefit from ABE completion more than lower risk offenders. [In a second study of 38 Ontario & Pacific region offenders who] participated fully in ABE and were released on full parole or mandatory supervision . . . (79%) were employed full-time and most had gained employment within the first month after release. . . . The survey data also suggested that the acquisition of numeracy skill may be particularly important in giving offenders a sense of self-mastery." The Motiuk, Boe & Cousineau paper (cited in part A) reports a study of "52 paroled offenders who participated fully in the prison industries program (CORCAN) [and] had a 27.8% reduction in re-admissions (from 26.6% for the benchmark group to 19.2% in the program group)."

v. What else? Along with rehabilitation programs, risk is, or can be, mitigated by ongoing offender assessment and corresponding placement: from maximum to medium to minimum security institution to community day parole to community release with high quality Intensive Supervision Probation by highly motivated & qualified staff until the risk to re-offend is judged to be negligible. As well, a release plan should be developed for the inmate released into a community where re-offence and re-addiction are unlikely, and employment is likely /available /pre-arranged. The assigned Probation Officer or Agency would monitor the offender's compliance with release conditions on an ongoing basis, providing assistance as required.

It is encouraging to note that virtually all of the rehabilitation elements outlined above are currently available within the

Canadian Federal Corrections System. Two key pieces are missing. The first is the consistent application of the above elements to every violent offender. The second is the release of any two or more time violent offender prior to rehabilitation.

D. REFERENCES

1. Andrews, D.A. & Bonta, J. *Psychology of Criminal Conduct (3rd ed.)* Cincinnati, OH. : Anderson, 2003.

2. Correctional Services of Canada. Counter-point accreditation case file. *Correctional Services of Canada Document*, 2004 (May).

3. Cortoni, F., Nunes, K. & Latendresse, M. An examination of the effectiveness of the Violence Prevention Program. *Correctional Services of Canada*, 2006 NoR-178.

4. Ettner, S. L., Huang, D., Evans, E., Ash, D. R., Hardy, M., Jourabchi, M., & Hser, Y. Benefit-cost in the California Treatment Outcome Project: Does substance abuse treatment "pay for itself"? *Health Research and Educational Trust*, 2005, DOI 10:1111/j.1475-6773.2005.00466.x.

5. Gendreau, P., Goggin, C. & Cullen, F.T. The effects of prison sentences and intermediate sanctions on recidivism. *Public Works and Government Service Canada*, 1999-3, JS42-87/199E.

6. Marsteller, F.A., Rolka, D. & Falek, A. Emory University evaluation of the Georgia DUI Alcohol/Drug Risk Reduction Program fiscal years 1992-1996. *Emory University*, 1997 (October 27).

7. Martineau, R. What works? Questions and answers about prison reform. *The Public Interest*, 1974 (June), *36*, 22-54.

8. Menninger, K. *The crime of punishment*. New York: Penguin, 1977.

9. Petersillia, J. Understanding California Corrections. *California Policy Research Center*, 2006.

10. Porporino, F.J. & Robinson, D. Can educating adult offenders counteract recidivism? *Correctional Service of Canada*, 1992 (January) Research Report No R-22.

11. Smith, P., Goggin, C. & Gendreau, P. The effects of prison sentences and intermediate sanctions on recidivism. *Public Works and Government Service Canada*, 2002-01, JS42-103/2002.

E. CONCLUSIONS & RECOMMENDATIONS

1. Conclusions: parts A&B The typical Canadian violent offender is a Caucasian male from a dysfunctional family where violence occurred. He has a personality disorder, was first arrested as a juvenile & has had multiple arrests, is a substance abuser, lacks a high school education, is unemployed & has an unstable job history, and is single.

The Canadian public has an appreciation that sub-optimal family home conditions are a major cause of crime, and has little faith in the ameliorative value of the criminal justice system.

1. Recommendations: parts A&B After the second conviction for a violent offence, the offender should not be released until he is assessed as rehabilitated. This will require changes to the criminal code, specifically legislation dealing with *Young Offenders* and *Dangerous Offenders*, and/or perhaps a new act for *Violent Offenders*. The data indicate that the '2 or more times' violent offender will continue to re-offend unless rehabilitated. This is not more punishment inflicted on the violent offender for his criminal behaviour; rather, it is recognition that he will continue to offend/ is unable not to re-offend until his violent tendencies are rehabilitated. With an 80-90% probability of re-offending, it is unfair both to the Canadian Public and to the Violent Offender to release him until his likelihood of re-offending is assessed as negligible. It is time to put a stop to the violence once a pattern – 2 violent offences is established!

As well, to implement these recommendations, closer coordination with the provinces will be required, as will the likely upgrading or a new classification of prison staff to a rehabilitation competence level, both federally & provincially. Where this is not feasible, enlisting the support of community-based rehabilitation services agencies would be required.

2. Conclusions: parts C&D The recidivism of the merely incarcerated is 80-90%, a glaring indictment of longer sentences as the answer to violent crime in Canada. 'Mere incarceration' is costly, ineffective, and unnecessary, since the federal justice

system has produced some highly effective methods of rehabilitation, methods which are already in the mandate of Corrections Canada.

2. Recommendations: parts C&D Ensure that all repeat violent offenders, without exception, leave penitentiary having completed a rehabilitation program that provides, as much as possible, for their successful re-entry back into Canadian Society. To achieve this requires that each repeat violent offender meets certain conditions: Completion of Violence Prevention Program, either the program described in Cortoni, Nunes & Latendresse's paper cited in part D, or some equivalent combination of anger management (described in Nafekh & Motiuk's paper cited in part D) and anti-social attitude adjustment (the Counter-Point Program) described in the Correctional Services of Canada study cited in part D.

Completion of Substance Abuse Program, as described in the Motiuk, Boe & Cousineau paper cited in part A.

Completion of required Education & Employment Programs, whether Adult Basic Education as described in the Porporino & Robinson report in part D, and/or prison industries program (CORCAN) as described in the Motiuk, Boe & Cousineau paper cited in part A, and/or some new education/employment initiative, e.g. high school completion, or trade school completion (carpentry, masonry/drywall, plumbing, electrical, mechanic, etc.).

The purpose of these 3 programs is to provide the violent offender with the requisite skills to make his re-entry into society a success. Violence Prevention should be required of all violent offenders, but substance abuse as well as education & employment programs should be conditional upon the needs of the offender. Prior to his release, he would be subject to ongoing assessment & appropriate placement: Maximum to medium to minimum security institution to community day parole to community release monitored by an Intensive Supervision Probation carried out by qualified & motivated corrections staff until the risk to reoffend is judged negligible. The release should be accompanied by a plan developed pre-release into a supportive community where the likelihood of re-offending & re-addiction is greatly reduced, and high likelihood of, or pre-arranged, appropriate employment. If Correction Services Canada lacks the staff resources to fully complete offender rehabilitation, the services of agencies such as Elizabeth Fry, John Howard & the Salvation Army could be used upon conditional release to fully complete the rehabilitation process.

There was an interesting article on page A11 of the March 23, 2007 The Globe and Mail of a gambling addict convicted of theft who requested, and was granted, a longer sentence, so she could have access to federal rehabilitation services. Many offenders know they need help to not re-offend. Informal discussions indicate the willingness of the vast majority of Canadians to provide the offenders not merely with incarceration but with effective rehabilitation that leads to a safer society with the ex violent offender a contributing member.

REFERENCES

Al-Anon. 2006. *Al-Anon Family Groups Welcomes Gays and Lesbians*. Virginia Beach, VA: Al-Anon Family Groups Inc.

Alcoholics Anonymous (AA). 1976. *Alcoholics Anonymous* ("Big Book"), 3rd ed. New York: Alcoholics Anonymous World Service Inc.

Arends, C. 2008. "The Grace of Wrath." *Christianity Today*, May, 64.

Associated Press. 2008. "Big quake to hit in next 30 years." In the *Barrie Examiner*, April 15, A7.

Barker, K., ed. 1985. *The NIV Study Bible: New International Version*. Grand Rapids, MI: Zondervan.

Bell, R. 2005. *Velvet Elvis: Repainting the Christian Faith*. Grand Rapids, MI: Zondervan.

Black, C. & L. Drozd. 1995. *The Missing Piece: Solving the Problem of Self*. New York: Ballantine Books.

Bly, R. 2004. *Iron John: A Book About Men*. Cambridge, MA: DaCapo.

Cann, R. L., M. Stoneking, and A. C. Wilson. 1987. "Mitochondrial DNA and human evolution." *Nature*, 31–36.

Cermak, T. L. 1989. *A Time to Heal*. New York: Avon Books.

De Haan, M. 2007. "Marital Abuse." *Been Thinking About*, October.

Dorit, R. L., H. Akashi, and W. Gilbert. 1995 "Absence of polymorphism at the ZFY locus on the human Y chromosome." *Science* 268: 1183–1185.

Douglas, J. D., ed. 1978. *The New International Dictionary of the Christian Church*, rev. ed. Grand Rapids, MI: Zondervan.

Dube, R. 2008. "Happy Marrieds, Take Heart." *Globe and Mail*, March 20, L1.

Eareckson, J. 1978. *Joni*. Grand Rapids, MI: Zondervan.

Eldredge, J. 2001. *Wild at Heart*. Nashville: Nelson.

Erikson, E. H. 1950. *Childhood and Society*. New York: Norton.

Govier, G. 2008. "Finders of the Lost Ark?" *Christianity Today*, May, 62.

Graham, B. 2006. *The Journey*. Nashville: W Publishing Group.

Hammer, K. 2008. "Toronto's white underbelly." *Globe and Mail*, May 17, M3.

Hendrix, H. 1990. *Getting The Love You Want*. New York: Harper.

Hsu, A. 2008. "A Multifaceted Gospel." *Christianity Today*, April, 66.

Johnson, C. K. 2008. "In the age of Prozac, fewer shrinks are doing talk therapy, study finds." Associated Press in *Globe and Mail*, August 5, L4.

Johnson, P. E. 1991. *Darwin on Trial*. Downers Grove, IL: Intervarsity.

"Just-Right Universe, The." 2007. *McGill In Focus,* Faculty of Science Edition. Montreal: McGill University, Fall, 12.

Kellogg, T. 1990. *Broken Toys, Broken Dreams*. Amherst, MA: BRAT.

Kesterton, M. 2008. "Bless This Divorce." *Globe and Mail*, April 28, L6.

Kubler-Ross, E. 1970. *On Death and Dying*. New York: Macmillan.

Kugel, J. L. 2007. *How to Read the Bible: A Guide to Scripture, Then and Now*. New York: Free Press.

Lewis, C. S. 1955. *Mere Christianity*. Glasgow: Fontana Books (Collins).

Miller, A. 1981. *The Drama of the Gifted Child*. New York: Basic Books.

Miller, A. 1990. *Banished Knowledge*. New York: Doubleday.

Moll. R. 2008. "Great Leap Forward." *Christianity Today*, May, 23–33.

Nouwen, H. J. M. 1992. *Life of the Beloved*. New York: Crossroad.

Olsen, R. E. 1999. "Don't Hate Me Because I'm Arminian." *Christianity Today*, September 6, 87–94.

Onions, C. T., ed. 1956. *The Shorter Oxford English Dictionary*, 3rd ed. London: Oxford University Press.

Packer, J. I. 2002. "What Happens to People Who Die Without Hearing the Gospel?" *Decision* (Canadian edition), January, 11.

Rawlings, M. 1979. *Beyond Death's Door*. Bantam: New York.

"Silencing of the lambs." 2008. *The Economist* print edition, May 8.

Stanley, C. 1988. "Brokenness—The Way to Blessing." *The Canadian Gideon*, July–August, 4–5 and September–October, 4–6.

Stanley, C. 1994. "What I Had Missed." *Moody Magazine*, December, 30.

Stanley, C. 2008. "Early Light." *In Touch*, January 8.

Strong, J. 1894. *The Exhaustive Concordance of the Bible*. Nashville: Abingdon.

Thaxton, C. B., W. L. Bradley and R. L. Olsen. 1984. *The Mystery of Life's Origins*. New York: Philosophical Library.

Tolle, E. 2004. *The Power of Now*. Novato, CA: New World.

Tozer, A. W. 1982. *The Pursuit of God*. Harrisburg, PA.: Christian Publications.

Tunstall, K. 2007. "Position Paper on Dealing with Violent Offenders so as to Really Make Canada Safer." Barrie, ON: Unpublished.

Virkler, M., and P. Virkler. 1991. *Communion With God Seminar Workbook*. Elmira, NY: Communication With God Publishers.

Yancey, P. 1990. *Where Is God When It Hurts?* Grand Rapids, MI: Zondervan.

Yancey, P. 1997. *What's So Amazing About Grace?* Grand Rapids, MI: Zondervan.

Yancey, P. 2000. "Lessons from Rock Bottom." *Christianity Today*, July 10, 72.

Yancey, P. 2008. "The Benefits of Brokenness." *Christianity Today*, May, 80.

Yancey, P. 2008. "The Dangers of Success." *Our Daily Bread*, September 7.

Zondervan Parallel New Testament in Greek and English: The Interlinear Greek-English New Testament. 1978. Grand Rapids, MI: Zondervan.

About the Author

Ken Tunstall has a BS & MS from McGill University and a PhD from the University of Toronto. His professions include computer programmer/systems analyst, university professor and management consultant. As professor and management consultant, he produced many professional writings.

Ken had a life-changing encounter with God at age 20 and experienced salvation at age 40. Over his lifetime, he has always had a significant involvement with the church, mostly the PAOC, the Roman Catholic Church and the United Church.

He's also a thirty-year student of the Bible and ten-year prison volunteer. Finally, he continues to enjoy life and being a child of God, father, grandfather and author.

Printed in the United States
129944LV00004B/517-615/P